DOCTOR DOG

M.R. WELLS

HARVEST HOUSE PUBLISHERS
EUGENE, OREGON

Cover by Harvest House Publishers, Inc.

Published in association with the literary agency of Mark Sweeney & Associates, Naples, FL 34135.

The information shared by the author is from her personal experience and the personal experience of others. It should not be considered professional advice. Readers should consult their own health care and dog care professionals regarding issues related to their own health and safety and the health, safety, grooming, and training of their pets.

All the incidents described in this book are true. Where individuals may be identifiable, they have granted the author and the publisher the right to use their names, stories, and facts of their lives, including composite or altered representations. In all other cases, names, circumstances, descriptions, and details have been changed to render individuals unidentifiable.

DOCTOR DOG
Copyright © 2016 by M.R. Wells
Published by Harvest House Publishers
Eugene, Oregon 97402
www.harvesthousepublishers.com

ISBN 978-0-7369-6465-4 (pbk.)
ISBN 978-0-7369-6466-1 (eBook)

Library of Congress Cataloging-in-Publication Data

Names: Wells, M. R. (Marion R.), 1948- author.
Title: Doctor dog / M.R. Wells.
Description: Eugene, Oregon : Harvest House Publishers, 2016.
Identifiers: LCCN 2015046923 (print) | LCCN 2016014930 (ebook) |
    ISBN 9780736964654 (pbk.) | ISBN 9780736964661 (eBook)
Subjects: LCSH: Dogs—Religious aspects—Christianity. | Human-animal
    relationships—Religious aspects—Christianity. | Dog rescue--Anecdotes.
Classification: LCC BV4596.A54 W443 2016 (print) | LCC BV4596.A54 (ebook) |
    DDC 242—dc23
LC record available at http://lccn.loc.gov/2015046923

Printed in the United States of America

16 17 18 19 20 21 22 23 24 / VP-KBD / 10 9 8 7 6 5 4 3 2 1

Salute to Skylee and Oki

This book is lovingly dedicated to all dogs and humans who work paw in hand to bring a healing touch. And to represent them, we salute Skylee and Oki. Golden retriever Skylee and German shepherd Oki were founding members of the American Red Cross K9 Action Team. They attended special military events and were a comfort to servicemen, servicewomen, and their families who were facing deployment or the stresses of reentry. Skylee and Oki moved on to their doggie reward during the writing of this book, but their memory lives on in the hearts they touched. To Skylee and Oki, their beloved humans, and all the other dogs and humans in these pages, thanks for being God's blessing!

Many Paws Make Light Work

Many hands (and paws) make light work, and this book is no exception. I am incredibly grateful to all who shared their stories in these pages. I am so blessed by my wonderful team at Harvest House Publishers, including my editor, Kim Moore, and my amazing agents, Mark and Janet Sweeney. Special thanks goes to Dottie P. Adams and Pastor Jim Leonard for their review and suggestions. Most of all, I am grateful to God, our Great Physician, the source of all healing, the One who designed us and dogs for each other. All praise and glory to Him, forever and ever!

Contents

Part I
Some Therapists Eat Kibble

Part IV
Pet More, Stress Less

Part V
Life Ends Better with a Dog

Introduction
D-O-G Spells Hope

One of my favorite words in the English language is *hope*. What a tower of meaning that tiny word carries! Hope propels us past seemingly insurmountable obstacles and lifts us from the pit to reach for the stars. Hope is a pinprick of light in the blackness; a set of steps in a sheer rock wall; an opening parachute in a plummeting free fall. And for some in this book's pages, hope has been a dog.

Dogs are a marvelous healing influence. They give hope by doing what humans can't or won't, and they delight to serve. Dogs are a help and a lifeline for children and adults with special needs. Dogs open bridges of communication to people stunned and numbed by crisis. Dogs coax responses from the sick and the aged that at times are nothing short of miraculous. Dogs walk with us through our hurt and pain, soothe our stress and anxiety, and offer a balm to those crushed by depression. And they do it all with gentleness and love.

It seems almost unbelievable until you consider who created dogs. How marvelous that the God of all hope chose dogs as a means to convey it. How like our God to make warm furry beings to lavish their love on us and, in so doing, make His love and care more real. And how encouraging to see His provision as He unwraps layer after layer of all the incredible ways He has designed dogs and us for mutual blessing.

I praise God for hope in Him that never fails. I delight to see His hand in this book's stories. And I pray that as you read about the healing touch of dogs, and God, your faith will be strengthened, as mine has.

Meet the Author's Pups

Becca, Marley, and Mica are a trio of pint-sized "toy joys" who are dearly loved furry companions and writing buddies.

Becca is a beautiful apricot-and-white Pomeranian fox. She loves to go "trick and treating," performing for goodies. She also loves giving doggie kisses and getting belly rubs.

Marley is a gorgeous sable-and-white papillon mix. He's the resident doggie "man of the house." He delights to watch over his women—canine, feline, and human. An empathetic little guy, he is right there with a comforting smooch if he senses his mom is upset.

Mica is a stunning sable-and-white poshie (Pomeranian/toy sheltie mix). She adores everyone and never met a four-foot she didn't want to play with. But her favorite partner in doggie crime is Marley. She could chase and wrestle with him all day.

Part I

Some Therapists Eat Kibble

💗 Zipporah 💗

The Giving Dog
God Gave Himself to Heal Us

The only gift is a portion of thyself.
RALPH WALDO EMERSON

Zipporah is a tiny Maltese with a titan of a heart for healing who delights to give of herself. Her giving journey began with a healing she herself received. She was a puppy then, and she loved to play. Her doting humans, Jerry and Hattie, treated her to toys, but one of them proved unsafe for her. Unbeknownst to them, she chewed off pieces of it and they lodged in her digestive tract. She got so sick one night that they had to rush her to the emergency vet. An X-ray showed her intestines were totally blocked. Zipporah urgently needed surgery, but by now it was almost morning, so her humans took her to her regular vet for the operation.

Jerry and Hattie have a strong faith in God. They prayed for their dog's healing. The vet, who happened to attend their church, scheduled the procedure for noon. Around 1:00 p.m., they got a call to come get their dog. They could not believe it was over and she was ready to be released. Turned out, the vet hadn't done surgery at all. He had taken one more X-ray to better pinpoint the blockage, and *there was no blockage. It was totally gone!*

The vet was stunned. This kind of obstruction normally didn't pass by itself. He had both X-rays, and clearly they were of the same dog. Zipporah weighed only four or five pounds. But her tiny intestines were totally clear, and she was no longer acting the least bit sick. Jerry and Hattie found her happily wagging her tail. To this day, Zipporah's vet calls her his miracle dog.

Soon the healing shoe would be on the other foot…er, paw. Jerry and Hattie wanted help in training their puppy. They signed Zipporah up with a woman who had a ministry training therapy dogs. She didn't charge for her services. Instead, she offered to work with Zipporah for free if her humans would take her to make hospital or nursing home visits. Deal!

Zipporah began her training at six months. She and Jerry were doing therapy work by the time she was a year old. Zipporah was incredibly well suited for it, and her humans saw God use her in some incredible ways.

Jerry still recalls the day they showed up at a hospital they often visited and found a note asking them to come to intensive care. Three or four doctors and some nurses were gathered in a circle. They explained that a patient had had surgery but had been unresponsive ever since. She was just lying and staring at the ceiling. They were worried she might be brain dead. They were only a couple of hours from starting a series of costly and extensive tests to determine if that was the case. But first they wanted to see if Zipporah could get any kind of reaction from her that might make those tests unnecessary.

Jerry gowned up and took Zipporah into the small room where the woman lay. He worked his way through a sea of machines and tubes until he was finally able to hold Zipporah up over the patient's head. He started calling the woman's name. "Brie? You have a visitor. Brie? Someone's here to see you."

The patient seemed unresponsive at first. Then Jerry noticed Zipporah was cocking her head, moving it left to right. He maneuvered around another piece of equipment to get closer to the woman and heard her making clicking sounds with her tongue. She was looking at Zipporah and had a bit of a grin on her face. Occasionally, she'd blink her eyes. Jerry glanced back at a window of glass behind him and saw the watching doctors literally dancing for joy.

After Zipporah had worked her magic with the patient, it was time to de-stress the doctors. They all held her, and one medic kept petting and petting her. Zipporah was so exhausted by how much she had given that she slept the whole next day.

Another patient Zipporah touched with her healing paws was a child, perhaps three or four years old. Jerry and his dog had been working awhile and were about to head home. A woman came up and asked if Zipporah was a therapy dog. Her little girl had been in and out of the hospital for about six months, and she'd become depressed and was just lying in her bed. But she loved animals. Would Jerry bring Zipporah to see her? Please?

Jerry knew he needed permission to take his dog into the area where the little girl was. He stopped at the nurses' station and got the go-ahead. He found the child in bed, arms attached to a board, needles sticking in her. Jerry talked to her a little, and then put Zipporah on the bed. The child tried to pet Zipporah with her foot. Jerry moved the dog up by the girl's hips and held her so the child could reach her. Within minutes she was up on her knees, petting Zipporah with both hands, one on either side of the dog. Zipporah let the little girl do whatever she wanted. A passing nurse saw what was happening and sang out, "Praise God! It's a miracle. Come see!"

Jerry and Zipporah stayed with the girl for more than 30 minutes. When they left, she was standing up, and all the nurses were looking in. Apparently she hadn't moved for a week.

Zipporah's heart for those who are hurting isn't confined to hospitals, and she seems to sense what they need. Jerry's wife, Hattie, has a friend with Parkinson's disease and Alzheimer's. When Zipporah is around her, she'll lay quietly on her lap. If she sees someone in a wheelchair at the mall, Zipporah wants to do the same thing—and will if permission is given.

Zipporah also seems to sense if someone is gravely ill, even when other humans may not. In one instance, Jerry and Hattie were having their RV repaired and spent some time at the shop where it was being done. Another couple was there as well. They seemed normal to Jerry and Hattie, but Zipporah kept lying beside the woman and acting like she did when she sensed something was wrong with a person. Finally, with some hesitation, Jerry spoke privately to the man and told him Zipporah seemed to think his wife had a problem. The man wept and told Jerry his wife had terminal cancer; she would probably live only another two or three months. Jerry and Hattie hadn't had a clue, but somehow Zipporah did.

Zipporah's healing touch is no longer focused on therapy work. Jerry and Hattie have been traveling a lot, which makes that difficult. But for the past few years, Zipporah has been Jerry's service dog. He has type 2 diabetes, and Zipporah has been trained to alert him to both high and low blood sugar levels. Just two days before Jerry and I spoke for this story, Zipporah woke him up at 3:00 a.m., licking his shoulder. He was extremely tired and was feeling okay. He ignored her, rolled over, and went back to sleep. Half an hour later she roused him again by licking the small of his back. This time he was having a night sweat. He got up and tested, and sure enough, his blood sugar was high.

Zipporah knows how to be a little lady when she's out in public. She understands that when her vest is on, she's working. Jerry attends a lot of meetings, and she can sit quietly for three or four hours and not make a sound. But when she's home and her vest is off, she lets her fur down and barks at what any dog would.

Thinking of Zipporah's heart for the hurting and their needs brings to mind Jesus's ministry when He walked this earth. Verse after verse in the Bible talks about how He had compassion on people and healed them. For example, in Matthew 14:13-14 we read,

> When Jesus heard what happened [Herod beheading John the Baptist], he withdrew by boat privately to a solitary place. Hearing this, the crowds followed him on foot from the towns. When Jesus landed and saw a large crowd, he had compassion on them and healed their sick.

Such healing, though, was just physical and temporary. It was but a picture of a deeper healing to come. Our giving God had sent His

Son, Jesus, our Messiah, to heal our terminal illness of sin when we least deserved it. Romans 5:6-8 (ESV) puts it this way:

> While we were still weak, at the right time Christ died for the ungodly. For one will scarcely die for a righteous person—though perhaps for a good person one would dare even to die—but God shows his love for us in that while we were still sinners, Christ died for us.

Jerry and Hattie know their giving dog is a gift from God, and they treasure her. But they treasure Jesus even more. They have gratefully received His healing. Have you?

Then he [Jesus] took a cup, and when he had given thanks, he gave it to them, saying, "Drink from it, all of you. This is my blood of the covenant, which is poured out for many for the forgiveness of sins" (Matthew 26:27-28).

Consider This:

How have others given deeply of themselves to help you heal? How might you do this for a person or pet in your life?

How Paws Mend Cracked Hearts
God Heals Our Brokenness

God uses broken things. It takes broken soil to produce
a crop, broken clouds to give rain, broken grain to give
bread, broken bread to give strength. It is the broken
alabaster box that gives forth perfume. It is Peter,
weeping bitterly, who returns to greater power than ever.

VANCE HAVNER

One of the world's most famous broken beings is a fictional egg. His story goes like this:

> Humpty Dumpty sat on a wall,
> Humpty Dumpty had a great fall.
> All the king's horses and all the king's men
> Couldn't put Humpty together again.

My friend Harmony isn't an egg, and she didn't fall off a wall. When her heart and life were shattered, she did not yet know her King, but He knew her plight and what was needed to help her heal. He sent not horses and men, but a dog.

From early childhood, Harmony lived in a broken situation. At one point, a boyfriend of her mother's abused her. When she was still a preteen, she and her younger brother were left alone for three months with only twenty dollars and a book of food stamps to sustain them. An older boy in the neighborhood started buying them food. She came to view him as her protector. He came from a broken situation too. At one point he moved into her mom's house. By the time she finished high school he had his own apartment and they started living together.

The relationship was abusive, but Harmony didn't see that clearly. She was more apt to recognize hurtful treatment of others than of herself. She was in college, studying psychology, but she didn't have a clear view of her own circumstances. What held a mirror up to her boyfriend's behavior and helped her view it in its true light was his treatment of a dog.

Chessie was a Staffordshire terrier. She was living with the boyfriend's mother. One day the mom had a stroke and landed in the hospital. Harmony and her boyfriend learned the dog had been left alone. Harmony had never been a dog person, but she had always loved animals, and she insisted they go and see about Chessie. They found her boarded up in the kitchen with no food or water, and her ribs were showing. Chessie came home with them.

Harmony became the one who fed and walked Chessie. She formed a close bond with the dog. Harmony's boyfriend isolated her from people, but she had Chessie, and the dog became her constant companion. Whenever things got really bad, she would put her four-pawed pal in the car and just drive. Chessie was extremely bright. Harmony felt she could talk to the dog as if she were a person. Instead of giving one- or two-word commands, she would say, "Chessie, I'm gonna need you to sit down now," and Chessie would.

Now years later, Harmony believes Chessie provided something special for her, something that was key to her ultimate healing. She has degrees in psychology and social work, and reflects that experts believe one significant factor in getting through trauma and having a positive outcome is the ability to form healthy, secure attachments. Harmony was able to form such a bond with Chessie at a time when she had no humans to provide that, and it made a huge difference.

Precious as Chessie was to her, Harmony didn't know how much she could count on her dog in danger. Chessie was sweet and mellow and often looked like she was smiling. When other dogs barked, she didn't react. Harmony wondered if Chessie would protect her, should the need arise. She learned the answer one night in dramatic fashion. She was alone with the dog that evening, and Chessie was on the bedroom floor beside her when she dozed off. She snapped awake in the wee hours to find Chessie standing over her chest. She was facing the window, barking furiously. Harmony heard a voice outside say, "Drop the knife. Let's go."

Harmony defended Chessie too. The dog was frightened of Harmony's boyfriend. If he wasn't happy with the dog's behavior, he could be mean. Harmony started to realize if he would treat a dog this way, he could do it to a child as well. Was this really the right person for her to be with?

After his mom's stroke, Harmony's boyfriend had pressured her to start working in a strip club to help make ends meet. Medical bills were piling up and money was tight. She did as he asked, but over time she began to have second thoughts about this too.

Ultimately, Harmony left both her boyfriend and the sex industry. He tried to keep Chessie, but she said, "No way!" Chessie remained with Harmony and lived to the ripe old age of 15 or 16, deeply valued and loved.

Chessie provided Harmony's first secure, healthy attachment, but Harmony's deepest relationship would be with God. She gave her life to Jesus, and He helped her understand how deeply and unconditionally she was loved and purposed. She was not only healed; she was transformed. She went on to found a ministry to women in the sex industry, to let them know how deeply God loves and values them. She and her staff have reached out to women all over the country and the world with the message of God's love, and have trained others to do the same. If women wish to leave the industry, they can come to her ministry for counseling and support. She has also written a book about her journey, *Scars and Stilettos: The Transformation of an Exotic Dancer*. The same God who sent Harmony a lifeline in fur to aid her healing process has not only healed and transformed her brokenness, but used her to help lead others to wholeness.

God has always brought healing from brokenness. When Jesus walked this earth He touched and transformed many shattered, suffering people. One such person was Mary Magdalene. We don't know a great deal about her, but Scripture tells us she had seven demons. From other passages describing what demons could do, we can only imagine the torment and isolation she suffered. After Jesus delivered her, she followed Him and was one of those who supported Him and His ministry. She was also among those who watched from a distance as He was crucified and saw His body laid in a borrowed tomb. When she returned to that tomb on the third day to finish anointing His body, it was gone, and two angels told her Jesus had risen. Then Jesus Himself appeared to her (John 20:1-18).

God used a dog to help Harmony heal. He cast demons out of Mary Magdalene. His means of mending are as individual as we are. No matter how badly broken we are, He can transform us into His choice vessels, pouring His love on others, if we give ourselves to Him.

The LORD builds up Jerusalem; he gathers the exiles of Israel. He heals the brokenhearted and binds up their wounds (Psalm 147:2-3).

Consider This:

Where in your life have you felt broken? Have you experienced God's healing? If so, how? If not, will you take your hurt to Him right now?

His Dog Lights Up His Life
God Guides Us to Healing

Hope, like the gleaming taper's light,
Adorns and cheers our way;
And still, as darker grows the night,
Emits a brighter ray.
OLIVER GOLDSMITH, "THE CAPTIVITY"

Allen and his black Labrador guide dog, Links, were at a bus stop not long ago when a little boy asked, "Hey, mister, is that a blind dog?" "I hope not, or we'd both have a problem," Allen told him. That's because Allen has only 15 percent of his sight and Links helps him safely navigate his surroundings. But that is only the beginning of this dog's healing influence. Links is also an emotional light offering love and companionship and brightening Allen's life with his very presence.

Links is actually Allen's third service dog. He got his first after being hit by a car. He was knocked into traffic and was almost hit again by a truck. He'd been considering a guide dog, and that accident propelled him into action. A big black Lab named John T. became Allen's eyes, succeeded after years of faithful service by a yellow Lab named Jolly. When age and arthritis forced Jolly to retire, Links took up the mantle.

Links came from a service dog organization called Leader Dogs for the Blind, and went through nearly two years of training. He knows about 40 commands and 60 words. Many of his words are locations, or places within a location, like the sauna at Allen's gym. Links not only helps his master get where he wants to go; he also pays attention to where Allen walks along the way. If there's a change in elevation, like a curb, Links will stop, cuing Allen that there's a problem and he needs to make an adjustment.

But what if Allen doesn't catch on or some unexpected hazard occurs? Links has been trained to step in and take matters into his own paws. This is called "intelligent disobedience." If he thinks Allen is headed for danger, he will refuse to budge. Should Allen try to override him or should some sudden danger loom, Links will cut in front of his human, block his way, and turn him around if necessary.

Recently, Links had to step in and take charge in the middle of a busy intersection near Allen's home. He couldn't see much, but witnesses filled him in afterward. "We were crossing when a car made a right turn on top of us," Allen told me. "Links did exactly as he was trained. He cut in front of me to stop me. Unfortunately he was not fast enough and the car grazed him. I could feel him getting squeezed between my leg and the car. Despite that and a bad crack on the head, Links safely guided me back to the curb. He definitely saved me from serious injury." Thankfully, this doggie hero sustained no permanent injuries, either, and after a few days off he was as good as ever!

Allen's dogs have widened his horizons in more ways than just getting around. It was partially thanks to John T. that Allen got a chance to help host a TV show called *Cooking Without Looking*. He and some other volunteers had agreed to be part of the studio audience, and as always, his dog went with him. Someone shone a light in his face and asked him how his guide dog assisted in the kitchen. "John T. helps with cleanup," Allen bantered. "If it's on the floor, it's his."

Maybe John T. got the goodies (only the safe ones, of course), but Allen got a hosting gig, thanks in part to his door-opening dog. Over the years, his guide dogs have also helped get their human to the studio on time. They've guided Allen in navigating the needed public transportation, and also helped him get around the studio set. If a person needed to take him somewhere, Allen pointed, said "follow," and his dog made sure they stuck with their guide.

Allen has loved doing the show, because it helps people who've lost their sight stay safer in the kitchen while doing more for themselves. "People who lose eyesight often lose independence," Allen told me. "The first time they make a mistake, they back off. We try to keep that from happening by teaching them helpful tricks." For example, people can learn to tell spices apart by smell. They can use differences in sound to grind coffee just right. If people have a little vision, choosing containers of different colors, shapes, and sizes for storage can help them distinguish one item from another. Raised dots can also be glued onto appliances like the microwave to help identify them.

At this writing, the show is available on YouTube and they also tweet and have a Facebook page. It was off the air for a while, but that is about to change. They will be shooting 13 new programs beginning in fall 2015, which will air on the on-demand Foody TV network and can be downloaded to smart TVs around the world.

Meanwhile Links has been helping Allen adjust to living in the adult community he moved into. Thanks to Links, Allen's never alone, and his dog is a great source of conversation, which makes him a big asset when it comes to meeting people.

Links and Allen's other dogs have also brought healing comfort to Allen in ways that are huge to him, though they might seem small to others. For example, Links is his computer buddy. Because Allen has limited sight, he is able to use a computer, but it's hardly a relaxing proposition. He has to work with his nose a foot from the screen and scan back and forth with his head to read, so his eyes have a tough time focusing. Thankfully, he has a program that can magnify print, tweak colors, and even read material to him. Still, it's a strain and he doesn't enjoy it one bit. What he *does* love is how Links trots over and curls up with his head on Allen's foot—a gentle, healing touch and reminder of his doggie love.

Thinking of Links and his healing influence on Allen's life brings to mind how the prophets ministered to the Israelites. God sent prophets to His people at various points in their history when they were about to get hit by a spiritual truck. They had stopped keeping His commandments and had fallen into idolatry, and they were in grave danger. God's prophets tried to guide His people back to Him. They shone the light of God's perspective on the people's sin. And they pulled the Israelites up short when there was a dangerous change in elevation on the spiritual path they were walking.

God's prophets also engaged in "intelligent disobedience." They did not submit to Israel's earthly rulers, even when their lives were in danger. They tried to turn those rulers—and the nation—away from evil, even when it meant rejection and persecution.

Links knows his job is to keep Allen safe, but he is only a dog. He can't be a healing influence unless Allen lets him. Nor could the prophets force the Israelites to heed them. God could force His ways on us, but He gives us free will even though our Great Physician longs to guide us to spiritual health through His Word, His Spirit, and His Messiah. If your spiritual vision is foggy and you're stumbling on life's path, reach for Him in prayer and ask Him to lead you, and He will.

In your unfailing love you will lead the people you have redeemed. In your strength you will guide them to your holy dwelling (Exodus 15:13).

Consider This:

Has someone ever stepped in front of you to block you and turn you from danger, either physically or spiritually? Did you heed them? What happened? How has God's guidance been a healing influence for you?

The Dog That Taught Acceptance
God's Insights Bring Healing

A weed is but an unloved flower.
ELLA WHEELER WILCOX

Mysti the Belgian Tervuren wasn't responding according to plan, and her human was miffed. Gale had had high hopes for her therapy dog. She aspired to do crisis response work, and went through extra training with Mysti so they could be a team.

Alas, Mysti didn't seem to be buying into Gale's dream. She was not all that good with other canines. Crisis response work involves multiple dog and handler teams working together, and that didn't seem to fit Mysti's personality. Gale struggled with this reality and with feeling as though her dog had somehow let her down.

Then, suddenly, a veil was lifted. Gale got smacked in the face by an insight she feels came straight from God. She realized she was repeating a pattern. Her own mother had always pushed her to be someone other than who she was. Now she was doing the same thing to her fur child.

Gale realized she had to be open to what Mysti needed in her life. It wasn't right to force her own agenda on her dog. Rather, she needed to tune in to Mysti's talents and find out what made her dog happy. Gale now says Mysti has been her greatest mentor, because her dog has taught her to embrace others for who they are and accept their capabilities and where they are in their lives.

God's insights sometimes take time to digest, and this one was no exception. Gale still wasn't quite releasing her crisis response dreams for Mysti. God had to give her an extra nudge. It happened when she and Mysti were involved in a mock trial of a crisis response situation. Mysti was exhausted and snapped at another dog while someone was petting her. Gale got the message and heeded it.

That was years ago. Mysti went on to do some wonderful therapy work that she enjoyed and was well suited for. Gale not only fully embraced her; she used the lessons Mysti had taught her to help guide other dog and handler teams. She has urged people she trains and mentors to tune in to what their dog wants and not force their pup into a mold that doesn't fit. She regrets she didn't do this for Mysti sooner, and tries to make it up to her every day.

Thinking of the insight God gave Gale through Mysti brings to mind the New Testament story of Mary and Martha. They were followers of Jesus and sisters of Lazarus. In Luke 10:38-42 (MSG), we read,

> As they continued their travel, Jesus entered a village. A woman by the name of Martha welcomed him and made him feel quite at home. She had a sister, Mary, who sat before the Master, hanging on every word he said. But Martha was pulled away by all she had to do in the kitchen. Later, she stepped in, interrupting them. "Master, don't you care that my sister has abandoned the kitchen to me? Tell her to lend me a hand." The Master said, "Martha, dear Martha, you're fussing far too much and getting yourself worked up over nothing. One thing only is essential, and Mary has chosen it—it's the main course, and won't be taken from her."

Mary and Martha had different gifts and talents. Different things made them happy. Martha was a doer. She was a first-century multitasker who loved entertaining and could keep many plates spinning at the same time. Mary was a thinker. She loved learning, especially about God, and would have happily sat soaking up spiritual truths for hours.

I believe Jesus dearly loved both sisters and embraced them for who they were. And I think He had two messages for Martha. Part of His intent was to caution her not to get so busy "doing" that she missed the joys of a relationship with Him. But I think He also wanted Martha to recognize, accept, and embrace her sister, Mary, for herself. Just as Gale learned to do for Mysti.

God loves each of us for ourselves, and He longs for us to love each other that way too. Will you ask Him to give you insight into where you may be falling short, so you can be healed and be used by Him to heal others?

The purposes of a person's heart are deep waters, but one who has insight draws them out (Proverbs 20:5).

Consider This:

Has God ever given you healing insights through your pets? What were they? How did they affect you and others? Are you struggling to embrace someone for who they are? Have you asked God to give you insight as to why?

It Took a Dog
God Unblocks Our Hearts

*You may be deceived if you trust too much, but you
will live in torment if you do not trust enough.*
FRANK CRANE

You may have heard the saying that it takes a village to raise a child.
But what if something goes terribly wrong with that village? What if
a young boy's stepfather abuses him? What if he gets beaten so badly
that he starts running away at an early age? And suppose he's in and out
of juvenile hall and gets labeled "incorrigible" by a judge who doesn't
understand?

And what if he's also dyslexic and can't read or write, and that iso-
lates him and bruises his heart and self-esteem even more? And then
suppose, as a young man, he joins the army to fight in the Vietnam War,
and his tendency to shut down his feelings is further heightened? And
because of all that and more, he develops a blockage of the heart that
he doesn't know he has, and that no surgery can remove?

That's what happened to my new friend John, but there was hope
for healing nonetheless. And it didn't take a village. It took a dog!

That dog was RJ, a female puppy who came into John's life at five
weeks of age. She was part shepherd, part sharpei, and part potluck.

John didn't care much for animals back then. But Pepper, the female he *did* care about, wanted her. Pepper's cousins had gotten the pup for their mom, who had just lost a dog. But Mom was still in mourning and wasn't ready to welcome a new four-legged friend. Pepper's cousins didn't have a fenced yard. So Pepper called John and asked if she could bring the pup to their house. John agreed, as long as Pepper did all the caring for the dog, because he didn't want much to do with it.

Pepper, a consummate animal person, was fine with that. RJ turned out to be a wonderful pup. In time, Pepper got her a trainer and took her to puppy classes. What she didn't quite realize was how RJ was getting under John's skin. One day when she was about nine months old, RJ jumped on the couch. This was not allowed. Pepper started to correct her, and John intervened. "If she's going to be both of ours, I want her on the couch like any other family member," he told Pepper.

From that moment, the die was cast. John was actually home more than Pepper, and he and RJ developed a special bond. RJ became John's window into a whole new world. He hadn't interacted much with children and animals. He wasn't all that good at developing deep relationships with people either. That was because of the invisible yet very present emotional wall he'd subconsciously built between himself and others. He was a professional musician, singer, and songwriter, and he could connect with an audience and with his fans. But personal relationships were different. He couldn't trust enough to let his guard down. RJ changed that.

RJ gave John a chance to care for someone other than himself. John could dare to have feelings for RJ that he'd never risked having for people. And John discovered that taking these baby steps with his beloved RJ allowed him to start taking risks with humans too.

One such risk involved John's mother. She had not abused him like his stepfather had, but she'd ignored the abuse and never told John she loved him. Pepper encouraged John to reach out to his mother, and he did. But he hadn't attempted any deep emotional connection. That changed one day when he was visiting his mother in assisted living. Emboldened by his growing emotional bond with his dog, John decided to take the plunge. As he was leaving that afternoon, he turned to his mom. "I love you," he said. She turned away, stared at the floor, and managed, "Yeah, I know."

That wasn't much, but John persisted. It took months, but finally his mom said, "I love you" back to him. It was an awakening for John. He started realizing if he opened up and shared his own heart and emotions, he could help others open up as well.

John and RJ didn't need any words to let each other know they cared. John recalls how they'd sit on the bed facing each other. John could feel his puppy's breath. They could feel each other's love.

RJ could also sense when John was down. He recalls taking his dog on a trip to a hot springs. They were staying at a little cottage. John was relaxing on the bed when he was hit by a wave of overwhelming depression. As he felt this, RJ snapped to attention and jumped up beside him. She got right next to John as if she knew, and his mood lifted.

RJ also seemed to sense when something wasn't right with others. Once she sounded off when a neighbor's small dog had gotten loose. As soon as the pup was safely home, RJ quieted down. In another instance, she alerted to trouble with a different neighbor. When no one could get a response at the house, someone called the fire department. They took the door off and found the woman on the bathroom floor, unable to get up. She'd been there for a day.

Thanks to RJ, John *has* gotten up, emotionally speaking. He used to suffer from severe depression and wartime nightmares, but no longer. These days he loves animals and kids and is excited to share himself with them. In fact, he loves people of all ages and they love him too. They enjoy coming over and hanging out with him and Pepper, and nothing brings him more joy.

As for RJ, after having her 14 years, 3 months, and 12 days, John and Pepper finally had to put her down on April 4, 2012. John told me it was the worst pain he'd ever experienced. But thanks to the healing difference RJ made in his life, he was able to get through it, and now he and Pepper share their home with a beloved rescue dog named Jazz.

As I thought about John and RJ, I was reminded of a certain famous biblical singer, songwriter, and musician. David, the author of most of Psalms and Israel's greatest king, had a very different life from John's, but he faced his share of mega-challenges too. And like John, he sometimes languished in a pit of depression. But he found a way out. In Psalm 40:1-3 (NLT) he wrote,

> I waited patiently for the LORD to help me, and he turned to me and heard my cry. He lifted me out of the pit of despair, out of the mud and the mire. He set my feet on solid ground and steadied me as I walked along. He has given me a new song to sing, a hymn of praise to our God. Many will see what he has done and be amazed. They will put their trust in the LORD.

One of my pastors spoke on this psalm recently. He pointed out that when we are in the depths of despair, we may not be able to see much of anything else. Our whole focus is on our pain. We can't see any hope in that pit. But something changed that picture for David. *God entered that frame!* And when God entered, the picture changed, David focused on the Lord, and his hope was restored.

In John's case, RJ entered his frame—but God did too. I'm not sure exactly what John believes, but he told me that, these days, he turns his problems over to the Lord. He also knows his creativity is God's gift, and if he tries to create his music in his own strength, he can quickly see the difference.

How about you? Are you in a pit? Are your problems filling your frame? You don't have to stay there, or find your own way out. God is waiting to step into your frame, fill it with His unconditional love, and give you a new song, just as He did for David and John.

I called on your name, LORD, from the depths of the pit. You heard my plea: "Do not close your ears to my cry for relief." You came near when I called you, and you said, "Do not fear" (Lamentations 3:55-57).

Consider This:

Have you ever shut off your emotions and walled yourself off from others? Why did this happen? How did it affect your life? If your problems are filling your frame, will you invite God in?

Paws That Unlocked Healing

God's Touch Is like No Other

A very little key will open a very heavy door.
CHARLES DICKENS, *HUNTED DOWN*

Sometimes people will do things for dogs that they won't do for humans, and that's why paws may open healing doors hands can't. Four such paws belong to a wonderful Belgian Tervuren named Mysti.

One patient Mysti helped was a stroke victim she and her human, Gale, met while doing animal-assisted therapy at a rehabilitation hospital. The stroke had affected one side of his body, including his arm. Therapy made his arm hurt, and he didn't want to do it.

That all changed the day his physical therapist spotted Gale and Mysti and saw that Gale had a tennis ball. She motioned the pair over and asked the man if he'd like to throw a ball for Mysti. There was a catch, though. He had to throw it with his bad arm.

The man agreed. It was a perfect match-up. Mysti loved that ball; it was the only toy she played with. She didn't care how or where the ball was thrown; she would always fetch it. In the beginning, when her new friend could only throw a short distance, Mysti would jump up and catch the ball in her mouth. The man was delighted. As time progressed and the man could throw it farther, Mysti retrieved the ball and put it on the patient's lap.

Mysti worked with the man once a week for a month. He never complained about pain while throwing the ball for her. He improved tremendously, and would even do rehab work when Mysti wasn't there. The man also wanted to know all about Mysti, and Gale was happy to share. Gale learned their new friend loved dogs and had one at home he was missing. Gale thinks these chats were beneficial to the patient too. He left the hospital after that month, and Gale doesn't know what happened later, but he had clearly made some significant progress.

Gale and Mysti also had the chance to work with autistic children, and once again, Mysti opened healing doors humans couldn't.

One little girl had gotten to the point where she wouldn't do anything anyone asked. Gale brought Mysti to meet her at her teacher's request. She loved giving Mysti treats, and Gale realized they could use this to motivate the child to work on her speech, which was tough to understand. She had to earn the privilege of giving the treat by first using her words to give Mysti a simple command.

In the beginning, Mysti couldn't understand what the girl was saying. Gale solved the problem by standing behind the child. When the little girl gave a command, Gale cued Mysti with a hand signal. Mysti would obey, and the child got to give her a reward. Gale and Mysti kept working with the girl, and she eventually improved to the point where hand signals were no longer needed.

This child would also get Mysti water, read to her, and do puzzles for her. She would select wooden puzzles of animals, put them together, and hold them up for the dog to see. The child's teacher was blown away. When her mother came in and observed, she cried.

Another child was believed to be non-educable. She had palsy and couldn't walk, so she sat in a wheelchair with a tray. But one thing she could do was throw a ball, though she had no control over how she threw it.

Mysti didn't care. She would retrieve the ball no matter where it went, even if she had to crawl under a desk. She would always bring it back and set it on the girl's tray. No one had ever taught Mysti to do this. The child's teacher said this activity was the absolute highlight of her time in school.

Gale let another autistic youngster groom Mysti with some special soft brushes she would bring for this purpose. One day, out of nowhere, the boy started counting his brushstrokes. He counted up to 50 on his own. He had never done this before.

Gale sees Mysti as a door-opener. She was able to unlock these patients and get them to do things that could be healing for them. God's Spirit does the same for us in the spiritual realm. He must open the door of our hearts so we can receive the healing gift of forgiveness for sin through faith in Jesus's death for us on the cross.

Scripture is filled with examples of this, but the one that jumps at me happened on Pentecost after Jesus's death. Jesus had commissioned the disciples to spread the good news of the gospel to the ends of the earth, but told them to wait for the empowerment of the Holy Spirit. Pentecost came 50 days after Passover and celebrated God giving the Ten Commandments to Moses on Mt. Sinai. The disciples had gathered together. Acts 2:2-4 relates what happened next.

> Suddenly a sound like the blowing of a violent wind came from heaven and filled the whole house where they were sitting. They saw what seemed to be tongues of fire that separated and came to rest on each of them. All of them were filled with the Holy Spirit and began to speak in other tongues as the Spirit enabled them.

The sound of the Spirit's arrival not only got the disciples' attention; it drew a crowd of others as well. In that crowd were godly Jews from different parts of the Roman Empire, and they spoke a variety of languages. Now they were hearing the disciples speak in their native tongues, even though they were all Galileans and clearly shouldn't have been able to do so.

God's Spirit had created a door-opening experience for this crowd. Now He empowered Peter, the same fellow who had denied Jesus three times, to preach a powerful sermon claiming Jesus was Messiah. Moreover, the crowd heard that message in their own languages, and three thousand came to faith that day.

God made us. He knows our hearts may be locked up in ways we don't suspect. That's why He has sent His Spirit to draw us to His healing. That healing isn't confined to a single point in time; it continues our whole lives. Will you let Him do for you what you can't do for yourself?

The Spirit himself testifies with our spirit that we are God's children (Romans 8:16).

Consider This:

Have you ever been willing to do something for a pet that you wouldn't do for a person? What was it? Did this open you up in a new way? Have you asked God's Spirit to open you up to His healing?

Nick of Time Nic

God Heals in His Timing

Healing is a matter of time, but it is some-
times also a matter of opportunity.

HIPPOCRATES

Nic's first mission of mercy seemed a bit premature for such a young puppy, but it was in the nick of time for a gentleman named Tony. He desperately needed all the love this golden retriever had to give. Nic (short for Nicodemus) actually belonged to Tony's daughter-in-law, Kris. She did therapy work with her dogs and Nic was her newest candidate. Since he was so young, she'd taken him along on the drive from her home in Virginia to New Jersey to move Tony to assisted living near her and her husband. His health was worsening and they felt this was best, but the day of the move, Tony mostly felt overwhelmed and distressed.

Enter Nic. At the tender age of 14 weeks, he sensed the need and responded with his whole puppy heart. This normally wiggly ball of fur climbed on Tony's bed and cuddled and napped with him while Kris packed up Tony's things. Nic was also Tony's comfort on the six-hour drive back to Virginia, and kept being there for his new pal over time. Kris visited Tony two days a week, and Nic always came along.

Eventually Tony was moved to a different facility he liked better, and he grew close to a small white dog that lived there. Kris was able to ease Nic out of the picture. But for many weeks, Nic was Tony's lifeline in fur.

Nic's ministry with Tony was both a confirmation of Kris's past choices and a portent of God's future plans for this pup. Kris had been forced to all but retire another therapy dog of hers, Malachi, who had severe hip problems. She'd tried to train up two older puppies, but neither one worked out. She had almost exhausted her options when she heard about Nic's litter. She reached out to the breeder, and this fine woman's heart was grabbed by Kris's work and the thought that a dog of hers could make such a difference. She bumped Kris to the head of the waiting list. When they were old enough, Kris met the puppies and temperament-tested all of them. Nic was last but went straight to the head of the pack. "I knew right away he was the one," Kris told me.

Nic has not only been there in the nick of time for Tony, but also for a wonderful young man named John-Mark. Kris met John-Mark when she started doing pet-assisted therapy twice a month at a facility that cares for the severely disabled. Kris works with patients in the pediatric wing, and John-Mark has remained there even though, at 21, he is a little past the official age limit.

John-Mark has Duchenne muscular dystrophy. He can move his head and hands, but has little motion in his body. He has a vent and gets around in a power wheelchair.

Initially, John-Mark's therapy appointments were with Kris and Titus, her seasoned older therapy dog. Nic just tagged along as part of his learning process. But Nic and John-Mark became friends, and magic happened. Nic had no fear of either John-Mark's vent or his wheelchair. His main concern was trying to give his new pal puppy kisses. As Kris watched Nic's tail wag around his new friend, and saw John-Mark's face light up with joyful smiles, an idea was born. She asked John-Mark, "Would you like to help me with Nic's training?"

John-Mark seized the opportunity, and it's hard to tell who's been more delighted, him or his young four-legged friend. Training Nic has given John-Mark new purpose, and Kris has loved finding creative ways to help him do as much of the training as possible despite his mobility challenges.

For example, Kris adapted John-Mark's wheelchair so he could "throw" a ball for Titus. She placed a tray on his wheelchair and positioned a makeshift ramp from the tray to the floor. Using a pancake turner, he was able to push a ball down the ramp for the dog to fetch. Big boy Titus would just scoop up the ball and drop it back on the tray.

Nic learned to fetch the ball, too, but being smaller, he crawled up the ramp to return it, often trying to sneak in a puppy kiss as well. Kris reinforced Nic's learning by giving him a treat. But she wanted John-Mark to be totally in charge and do it all, and she found the answer in the form of a remote control treat dispenser. Now John-Mark can press a button on the remote with his thumb and deliver Nic's reward himself.

John-Mark is also teaching Nic to retrieve clothing items. Kris takes a shoe or a sock and puts it somewhere in the room. John-Mark tells Nic, "Get it!" Nic retrieves the item, jumps on a chair next to the wheelchair, and drops the clothing on John-Mark's tray.

Under the guise of puppy training, John-Mark and Nic are doing far more. They are building a bond of joy and trust. Nic proves to John-Mark every time they're together that he can leave a legacy and make a difference despite his challenges. John-Mark makes it fun and rewarding for Nic to go the extra mile with someone who needs him to. For example, usually young pups need hand signals as well as words to learn. John-Mark can't use hand signals, but Nic has been willing to focus on the verbal. Nic makes great eye contact, looking straight at John-Mark. Once a workman was present and distracted Nic when John-Mark was giving a command. But because of their closeness and trust, Nic quickly refocused and obeyed after Kris asked John-Mark to repeat it.

Kris sees a positive difference in John-Mark from working with Nic, and she's not alone. His recreational therapist, Danielle, feels it has provided an emotional boost. "I have noticed he's more vocal and he seems to trust himself more. His confidence is much higher than when I first met him," she said. "John-Mark smiles more when he is with Nic and when he is the one training Nic. He says he looks forward to Thursdays, when Nic is here. You can tell that by his body language. When Nic is here he really takes initiative to be on time for his sessions." Danielle also noted that John-Mark's family is proud of what he is doing with his favorite pup.

As well they should be. Kris got some heartwarming confirmation of the impact John-Mark is having when Nic worked a special needs conference. "Nic went to everyone, adult or child, who came by in a wheelchair," she told me. "A woman on foot and a young man in a wheelchair came through the door at the same time. The lady called to Nic and he totally ignored her. Instead, he went to the man in the chair, even though the man never called him at all. I believe John-Mark has built in Nic a relationship with anyone in a wheelchair. It is a heartwarming thing to watch and a marvelous legacy."

Recently Nic passed a test that makes him an official therapy dog, but his training, and his training with John-Mark, continues. As they share and grow, who knows how much healing their special partnership may ultimately bring?

When I titled this story "Nick of Time Nic" I was speaking from a human perspective. From God's perspective, the view is very different. God is outside of time and space, and He is sovereign over everything, including humans and puppies and healing. From God's perspective, Nic stepped into Tony's and John-Mark's lives in His perfect timing to accomplish His purposes, as Jesus did with Jairus's daughter (Luke 8:40-56).

Jairus was a leader of his synagogue. He came to Jesus begging for his young daughter's life. Scripture tells us she was about 12 years old and she was dying. She seemed beyond human help, but her father believed Jesus could heal the child he adored. If Jesus hurried, He might just get there in the nick of time. Jesus set out with the frantic dad, but a woman who had suffered 12 long years with a bleeding problem touched Him. Despite the life-and-death mission He was on, despite the large crowd that surrounded Him, Jesus stopped, determined to draw out this woman and minister to her.

Even before He had finished this task, word arrived that Jairus's daughter was dead. Humanly, it would seem that Jesus missed His window. All hope was lost, right? Not at all! Jesus was sovereign not just over sickness, but over death, and His timing was perfect for His purposes. He urged Jairus to believe, proceeded to the man's home, and in the presence of a select group consisting of the girl's parents and Peter, James, and John, raised Jairus's daughter from the dead. One can only imagine the additional spiritual healing that took place in Jairus's family and those three disciples that day, not to mention the ongoing impact of this story in Scripture.

So where does that leave us with the time constraints of this life? I believe we must work within them, but look beyond them. We must remember that God is not limited by our earthly constraints and boundaries, and His healing comes in ways and time frames we may not expect. Nic's healing touches with John-Mark and Tony are but one example of this. It's not Nic's timing at work here; it's God's—and healing may happen in eternity that doesn't take place in this life—which is why we must put our trust and hope in Him, just as Jairus did.

There is a time for everything, and a season for every activity under the heavens (Ecclesiastes 3:1).

Consider This:

Have you or someone you love ever experienced healing "in the nick of time"? Who was involved? What happened? Looking back, can you see God's hand and timing in the situation? Are you facing something now that you need to commit to God's timing, not yours, and put your hope for healing in Him?

The Paws That Held a Heart
God Makes Healing Connections

*What a grand thing, to be loved! What
a grander thing still, to love!*
VICTOR HUGO

Gale speaks of Annie as her "heart dog." They were so intertwined it was as if they were two chambers of a single heart. Annie healed Gale in a way no other living being could, and her impact will remain forever.

When they first met, the one in desperate need was Annie. She was just a puppy then. Gale's teenage son was working at a restaurant and a coworker had found the frightened German shepherd mix. He was moving and needed to park her somewhere for a night or two. Gale agreed to take her.

Annie was driven over in a van. She was cowering under the seat. The only way they could get her out was to take the seat out first. Gale gathered the shaking puppy into her arms—and knew right then that this dog needed to be hers. Her son asked his friend if Gale could keep her, and the boy was fine with it.

That first night, Annie lay motionless on a towel under the kitchen desk. When Gale took her out to do her business, she raced frantically around the yard. Her new humans got her a harness because she could not be on leash; she'd flip around and do circles in the air.

Thus began a bond that lasted for the next ten years. Gale described hers and Annie's relationship as the most profound unconditional love in both directions. Loving Annie showed Gale the depths of affection she could have for another living being. Their love was also characterized by exquisite gentleness—which is the piece Gale misses most.

For Annie, Gale was her world. Gale doesn't know what early terror Annie may have endured, but she was the only person Annie trusted completely until the very end of her life, when she reached a paw out to Gale's husband.

It may have been Annie's deep and desperate need for her human that worked a healing miracle in Gale's life. Gale believes God sent Annie to heal her heart. At the point when Annie showed up, Gale had been battling depression for years and needed to take medication for it. Something about their deep connection, Annie's desperate need for Gale, and her love and tenderness began to have a healing effect. Annie became Gale's confidant. She would pet Annie, love her, and talk to her.

"God uses many vehicles to heal us," Gale told me. "God made His love and tenderness real to me through a dog named Annie. She became the embodiment of His unconditional love." The results were nothing short of life-changing. Gale has been off her medications for five or six years now and attributes at least some of her improvement to Annie's influence.

God used Annie to paint a portrait of His love and gentleness for Gale and lift her spirits on the wings of love. Jesus used the parable of the prodigal son (Luke 15:11-32) to paint a picture of God's love and tenderness for His first-century hearers, and for us.

The prodigal son didn't love his father the way Annie loved Gale. His world did not revolve around his parent. In fact, he wanted nothing but to get his inheritance and go off to see the world. His dad knew he would get into trouble, but with a breaking heart, he gave his boy what the son desired.

The prodigal made bad choices. He went through his money. He wound up destitute and starving in a foreign land. One day he realized his father's hired hands were far better off than he was, and he decided to go home and beg to become one of them. He didn't know if his dad would let him do so, but he could ask.

What he didn't begin to fathom was the depth of his father's love. Though his son had rejected and deserted him, this loving father was constantly watching and waiting and longing for his boy's return. When at last the day came when he saw the prodigal approaching, he pulled out all the stops in his gentle and tender welcome of his long-lost child. He actually threw a welcome-home party for the boy!

There was also an older boy, and he didn't get it at all. He was offended that he had stayed home like a dutiful son, but his dad had never made such a fuss over him. At this point the older son, more than the younger, needed healing. He hadn't truly grasped the nature of his father's love. He didn't realize this love was not ignited by his children's performance, or quenched by their failings. He didn't realize he could have had a party too. He didn't "get" that their father was waiting to embrace them both and all he had to do was run into those waiting arms.

The father in this parable is a picture of God. He loves us with a depth of gentle, tender, unconditional love no human being can fully comprehend in this life. He gave Gale a glimpse of that love through a precious "heart dog" named Annie. Even as she gathered Annie into her arms and heart, God gathered her. Will you let Him gather you into His embrace?

I pray that you, being rooted and established in love, may have power, together with all the Lord's holy people, to grasp how wide and long and high and deep is the love of Christ, and to know this love that surpasses knowledge—that you may be filled to the measure of all the fullness of God (Ephesians 3:17-19).

Consider This:

Has the love of a pet or person ever given you a deeper glimpse into God's love for you? What happened? How did it help to heal and change you? How might you love and care for others in a way that helps them grasp God's love more deeply?

The Dog That Helped a Dream Come True
God Heals Our Disappointments

We all have our own life to pursue, our own kind of dream to be weaving, and we all have the power to make wishes come true, as long as we keep believing.

LOUISA MAY ALCOTT

He was a good dad, a caring dad—but he couldn't help feeling disappointed. He had always hoped that one day he'd play ball with his kids. But his daughter was born with special needs and challenges that made a game of catch between them seem like an impossible dream.

Little did this father guess that God would redeem that dream through a caring dog and human—and a baseball shirt. The dad was wearing that shirt when he dropped his daughter off for respite care at McLean Bible Church. He was not from the area. He'd come to attend a conference and was taking advantage of a program the church had in place. Two Saturdays a month, the families of kids with special needs could drop them off for skilled care while they took a much-needed break.

Kris and her therapy dog, Titus, were working with the children that day. She saw the man's shirt and they started talking. He shared his heart. She asked if he and his daughter had ever played toss. No, they hadn't.

After the man left, Kris got to thinking. Titus, a golden retriever, was a "ball dog." He absolutely loved playing ball, and she used this fact a lot when doing therapy with both children and adults. Maybe, just maybe, there was a way to make this dad's baseball dream come true. She only had a day with the girl, but she had God to call on for help, a God for whom nothing is impossible.

Kris began by standing in front of the girl and throwing the ball to Titus. She did this again and again as the girl watched. Eventually Kris handed her the ball. She sort of tossed the ball to the dog. Kris got the girl to repeat this numerous times. She moved the three of them all around the room that day. The girl kept throwing. Finally, the dad came back.

"I've almost got your baseball girl," Kris told him. She explained how she'd gotten his daughter to toss a ball to the dog. "Stand next to Titus," she coached the dad. "When your daughter throws the ball, I will tell Titus to leave it, and you catch it."

Titus was perfect, remaining in a down stay while the father caught the ball. Kris had him hand the ball to his daughter. Then Kris placed him next to Titus again. Titus moved behind the dad and his daughter threw her father the ball. Tears rolled down the father's face.

Kris gets a lump in her own throat when she recalls this experience. She feels it was a "God thing" that the dad mentioned baseball to her. She had the privilege of being involved in giving him a precious gift. God used Kris and Titus to redeem a father's dream. Perhaps not in the way he originally envisioned it, but I have to think in a way that was healing to his heart.

Thinking about this dad and his daughter brings to mind another father, one who pleaded with Jesus for his son (Mark 9:14-29). The son was possessed by an evil spirit. He couldn't speak and he had convulsions, gnashed his teeth, and foamed at the mouth. The dad had asked Jesus's disciples to free the boy, but they couldn't deliver. Just imagine what dreams this man must have had before his son was born. Just imagine how shattered those dreams, and that father, would have been.

This affliction had been going on since the boy was little. The dad was at his wits' end. "Have mercy on us and help us, if you can," he begged Jesus (Mark 9:22 NLT).

This man had clearly heard about Jesus and His healing powers. His dream now was for his son to be well. He was hoping Jesus could do this, but on some level it was still an "impossible dream." Jesus had an interchange with the dad about this.

"What do you mean, 'If I can'?" Jesus asked. "Anything is possible if a person believes." The father instantly cried out, "I do believe, but help me overcome my unbelief!" (Mark 9:23-24 NLT)

Jesus went on to cast out the spirit, heal the son, and make that father's dream come true.

So what can we learn from this tale of two dads? I believe both situations show that God redeems our dreams and heals our disappointments. But He does it in different ways in different people's lives. We don't all get the dream we envisioned, but He will work all things for our good and His purposes if we will put our trust in Him (Romans 8:28).

Do you have an "impossible dream" that has made your heart heavy with disappointment? Will you give it to God in prayer? Will you ask Him to heal and redeem it in the way He knows is best? Trust in the God who loves and cares about you more than you could ever begin to fathom and watch what He will do!

Kings will be your foster fathers, and their queens your nursing mothers. They will bow down before you with their faces to the ground; they will lick the dust at your feet. Then you will know that I am the LORD; those who hope in me will not be disappointed (Isaiah 49:23).

Consider This:

Has God ever healed a deep disappointment in your life, or redeemed what seemed an impossible dream? What happened? How did it change your life and your relationship with God? Is there a dream or disappointment you need to give to Him right now?

Their Bright Spot Was a Dog
God Gives Us Healing Moments

Making one person smile can change the world—
maybe not the whole world, but their world.

AUTHOR UNKNOWN

Sometimes marvelous things can happen in mere moments. Working with therapy dogs has taught Chris that. Like the day he and his golden retriever, Stormy, had an unusual encounter at a mental health facility. They had just come out of a group session where Stormy offered doggie love and support. Chris spied a tiny woman with an eye patch walking down the hall. When she saw Stormy, she started crouching lower and lower as she made her way toward him. By the time she reached the dog, she was on her knees. She wrapped her arms around Stormy's neck and hugged him.

Staff members rushed toward them, worried she was hugging Stormy's neck too tightly, but Chris realized she was doing him no harm. He stepped in to reassure them and gave the woman one of Stormy's stickers with his photo on it.

That might have been the end of the matter, but it wasn't. Evidently the woman was released soon after. A few days later, a staff member told Chris he'd seen that same woman in town, proudly wearing Stormy's sticker for all to see.

Chris can't know what overall impact Stormy might have had on this patient, but it's a good guess he was a bright spot in her day. And if you've got emotional struggles darkening your world, that kind of bright spot can be a wonderful healing moment. Chris and his dogs, Stormy, Daisy, and Ty, have made it their mission to offer such bright spots to some of those who need them most.

The aforementioned mental health facility is one place they do this. All three dogs have interacted with patients in a group setting. Each dog brings its own unique personality. Some patients have a dog at home or have had dogs in the past, and they're drawn to Chris and his dogs 'cause they miss their own. Some do a quick meet and greet and drift away. But others open up and start talking, sharing how dogs have helped and telling parts of their life story.

Stormy was making such a visit when, instead of making the rounds, as was his habit, he zeroed in on one particular patient. Chris was blown away to learn later that the patient in question was depressed and upset. Stormy had gone straight to the one who needed him most.

It has been so rewarding for Chris to hear he made someone's day better by showing up for an hour with a dog. Patients actually start crying because they're so happy to see the pups, and for some, a four-pawed presence helps them sit and listen. They look forward to these canine visits, and the staff has given Chris letters and cards left for him by patients' loved ones, telling him he and his dogs made a difference.

Chris's wife, Joan, works with the dogs too, and has taken Daisy on visits to the Alzheimer's side of an assisted living facility. One day Joan and Daisy walked up to a woman in a wheelchair who hadn't spoken in two years. Daisy put her head on the woman's lap and she started talking about the dogs she used to have. She was speaking intelligible words and seemed to know what she was saying. It didn't last long, but it was a bright spot nonetheless.

These special golden retrievers have also given "golden" healing moments to kids. Joan took Ty to visit a group of children with traumatic brain injury (TBI). Two of the girls were eager to throw a ball for the dog, but Ty focused on a boy who was showing signs of interest. When the girls finally threw the ball, Ty mouthed it, bypassed them, and plopped it on the boy's lap. The boy dropped it, but Ty and Joan refused to give up. Joan would throw it in the boy's stead, and Ty retrieved it again and again. At last, when Ty dropped the ball at his feet, the boy picked it up and threw it to the dog himself.

Another time a local homeless shelter invited Chris to bring a dog over. He chose Stormy to go. When they started up the walk, a group of 10 or 12 children came running out the door, but pulled up short about 50 feet away and shrank back inside. Later, after Chris had checked in, he put Stormy in a down stay and the kids crept closer little by little. They were crawling all over Stormy and lying on him by the time Chris left.

When I think of healing moments and the impact they can have, it brings to mind what God can do in a moment. In his first letter to the Corinthians, Paul points out that our final bodily resurrection will be every bit that fast.

> Let me reveal to you a wonderful secret. We will not all die, but we will all be transformed! It will happen in a moment, in the blink of an eye, when the last trumpet is blown. For when the trumpet sounds, those who have died will be raised to live forever. And we who are living will also be transformed. For our dying bodies must be transformed into bodies that will never die; our mortal bodies must be transformed into immortal bodies (1 Corinthians 15:51-53 NLT).

In a moment, a dog can transform a person's day. In a moment, God can transform us for eternity. It is the size of our God, not the size of the time frame, that matters in the end. Never discount the healing impact you may have on someone in a moment or the eternal benefits it may bring.

Jesus turned and saw her. "Take heart, daughter," he said, "your faith has healed you." And the woman was healed at that moment (Matthew 9:22).

Consider This:

When was the last time a pet or person changed your world through a healing moment? What happened? Why did it have such an impact on you? Did it bring ongoing benefits? What healing moments might you offer others?

The Listening Dog
Listening to God Brings Healing

Skillful listening is the best remedy for loneli-
ness, loquaciousness, and laryngitis.
WILLIAM ARTHUR WARD

Tye is a dog who loves kids and listens to them with both his ears and his heart. And that's why some who come to read to this empathetic golden retriever receive healing touches no one expected.

Being a reading dog wasn't the calling Tye started out with in life. He was being groomed to be a service dog for a child with special needs. A marvelous nonprofit, 4 Paws for Ability, had him in training and was going to match him with a youngster when he was ready. Then when he was 14 months old, he was diagnosed with hip dysplasia, and they weren't sure he'd be able to fulfill such duties. They put him up for adoption instead, and at 15 months of age he went home with a brand-new adult forever friend named Mare.

When Mare saw Tye's love for kids and awesome temperament, she decided she just had to share him. Maybe he was meant not just for one child, but for many. She had him trained, tested, and certified as a therapy dog, and they both got additional training to do reading with kids.

At one particular library, Tye has a blanket on the floor. Kids sit with him and read him stories. He knows he's working and he also seems to sense when one of his young charges needs a special touch. Now and then he'll put his head on a child's lap. He also has an endearing way of putting his paw on a book page.

Mare and Tye visit schools as well, where Tye works his listening magic. Kids who can't read in front of other people will read to Tye. One little boy couldn't even sit with Tye and Mare when they first started coming. He'd had some devastating trauma and loss in his life. Over time he began to warm up and would take a book to Mare. She would read it for him, and he would point to the words. Meanwhile he would be petting Tye. This child's teacher thanked Mare and told her, "You don't know what you've done for this boy. He has come so far!"

Another child, a little girl, had behavioral problems. She had attention deficit issues and would hit herself. She was a good reader, but some days she wouldn't want to read at all. She seemed to be having a bad day and would just want to hold Tye. Mare never asked what the problem was, but the child would cuddle up close to Tye and start telling him what was wrong. After doing that she'd be better and she'd kiss Tye and thank him.

On the academic side, two teachers in particular have told Mare that she and Tye are making a difference. Their pupils are reading more fluently. They are also raising their hands more and participating more in class. These teachers feel the reason is reading time with Tye.

Tye reaches out to kids at home too. When one young relative of Mare's is having a pout, she'll hide behind a chair, right where the chair back meets the armrest. Tye pushes her head with his nose till she lifts it up and laughs.

Nor is Tye's empathy limited to hurting children. When Tye had been with Mare less than a week, a big storm hit. Mare had an older golden retriever who was scared of everything, and he was terrified. Tye lay on a blanket by his side till his new doggie big brother fell asleep. And more recently when another relative showed up with a tooth so painful she slumped in a chair in tears, Tye jumped up on the chair next to hers and tried to lick those tears away.

Tye brings a healing touch to others by "listening" and reaching out.

But he doesn't force the issue. Those he's helped also made a choice to receive what he was offering.

Infinitely more than Tye, God knows each of our pains and struggles. He also reaches out in a multitude of ways. But we can choose whether to receive the healing He offers, and part of that choice involves *listening to Him.*

Scripture is filled with examples of this, but I was captured by the Old Testament story of a prophet named Balaam. An evil Moabite king named Balak sent emissaries to hire the prophet to go to him and curse the Israelites. God said, "Don't go!" But when Balak sweetened his offer and sent his emissaries back, Balaam's heart was to listen to the Moabite king and not to the King of Creation. God told Balaam, "Since these men have come to summon you, go with them, but do only what I tell you" (Numbers 22:20). Balaam "heard" God say okay, but did not "listen" to pick up on His displeasure.

It took a donkey and the angel of the Lord to start turning Balaam around. The donkey dodged the angel twice before finally balking and lying down in the road, despite being beaten by Balaam. Then God gave her human speech so she could protest. "Am I not your own donkey, which you have always ridden, to this day? Have I been in the habit of doing this to you?" (Numbers 22:30)

Then God made the angel of the Lord visible to Balaam, and he really listened to what the angel of the Lord said. He got the message that he had displeased God and the donkey saved his life. I have to think that some spiritual healing was taking place, because Balaam got really committed to telling King Balak exactly what God told him to say.

Balaam proceeded to deliver to Balak three messages blessing the Israelites, which was just the opposite of what Balak wanted. At this point the enraged pagan king ordered Balaam to go home. But Balaam listened to God, not Balak, and refused. He delivered four more messages warning what Israel would do to its enemies in the future.

God spoke to Balaam through a donkey and the angel of the Lord. Today He speaks to us through His Word and His Spirit. Is there an area of your life where you've been "hearing" Him but not really listening? God knows and loves His children infinitely more than Tye does his. Why not listen as Tye does, with not just your ears but your heart, and see what healing He may bring?

He said, "If you listen carefully to the LORD your God and do what is right in his eyes, if you pay attention to his commands and keep all his decrees, I will not bring on you any of the diseases I brought on the Egyptians, for I am the LORD, who heals you" (Exodus 15:26).

Consider This:

Was there a time when you felt really listened to by a person or a pet and it made a healing difference? What happened? How did it change your life? What might help you listen more carefully to God going forward?

A Paw Across the Chasm
With God, No Healing Is Impossible

Miracles are not contrary to nature, but only
contrary to what we know about nature.
Saint Augustine ·

If we believe God made everything, and knows everything, and we humans don't, it shouldn't surprise us when things happen that we don't understand. That's why Ginny hasn't been surprised at the healing miracles her pet therapy golden retriever, Molly, has had a paw in.

One situation involved a girl who had been in a coma for three weeks following a skiing accident. Ginny and Molly visited her in the hospital. Ginny took the girl's hand and used it to pet Molly, all the while speaking to the youngster. "This is Molly. She's a pet therapy dog," Ginny told her. At the time, there was no response. But half an hour after Ginny left, the girl's eyes fluttered and she spoke and asked to see the pup.

The hospital got in touch with Ginny. By the time she and Molly returned the next day, the girl was out of bed. She was able to pet Molly on her own and say a few words. She went on to make a full recovery, and she remembered stroking Molly while she was in the coma.

In another situation, Ginny and Molly spent time with a woman in ICU who'd been in a motorcycle accident. She was bandaged head to toe like a living mummy, and didn't open her eyes. Her mom was with her and tried to help her pet Molly. Only the injured woman's fingertips were uncovered. The mother used those fingertips to stroke Molly's fur while explaining that Molly was a pet therapy dog. Ginny and Molly visited this woman once a week for a month. She seemed unresponsive the first couple of times. Ginny thinks she might have been heavily sedated, but she doesn't know for sure. What she does know is that eventually the woman began to talk, and she recalled petting Molly on those earlier visits.

Molly also lent a healing paw in a local hospital's behavioral health unit, which was a lock-down facility. Ginny took her dog to the teen section quite a bit. She remembers one boy in particular who was staring at the wall, glassy-eyed. When he saw Molly, he came over, knelt down, and began petting her. Then he actually started to smile. The therapist said this was the first response anyone had gotten out of him since he arrived.

Lots of the teens loved Molly there. When they saw her, they came running over. They told Ginny, "Oh my goodness, this is making me happier than anything!"

Nor was Molly's healing touch limited to the teens in the unit. To get to them, Ginny had to travel through an adult section. One day a young man in his early twenties ran out of a room and intercepted Ginny. "Please come in and see my roommate," he pleaded. The roommate was sobbing because he missed his dog so much. Ginny brought Molly in, and the roommate was thrilled. Molly jumped up on the bed on a clean sheet they put down for her, and the sobbing man wrapped his arms around the dog. He told Ginny how grateful he was, and that seeing Molly had made his day bearable. "You are an angel sent from heaven!" he exclaimed.

As I was thinking about all these incidents, I detected a common thread. In every case a human needing healing was somehow separated from those trying to help, and a dog reached its paw across that chasm and connected. There was also a chasm separating the son of the Shunammite woman from his loved ones, and the prophet Elisha reached across it and brought him back from death.

The story is found in 2 Kings 4:8-37. Elisha was making trips to Shunem and a wealthy woman in that city reached out to him and helped him. She recognized he was a holy man and extended hospitality to him. She even prevailed on her husband, and they made a room for Elisha on their roof so he had a place to stay whenever he was in their area.

Elisha wondered what he could do for her. The prophet's servant pointed out that the woman had an aging husband and no son. She didn't quite believe Elisha when he told her she would give birth to a boy the next year. But she did indeed have a son, just as Elisha had promised. And then, when the child was a few years old, one day he went out to the fields during harvest, got a terrible headache, and died on his mother's lap.

The mother refused to accept the boy's death. She laid him in Elisha's room and rushed off to find Elisha and enlist his help. Without going into all the details, Elisha hurried to the boy, prayed to God, and through God's power, brought him back to life.

It's important to note that Elisha didn't raise the boy in his own strength. He prayed and reached across death's chasm in God's strength. The Bible teaches that all life is from God. God gave life when the boy was conceived, and again when he was raised from the dead.

What a picture of the healing we all need! We need God to give life in the womb, but we also need Him to heal us from the spiritual death of sin. This is the tallest healing order there is, but no healing is impossible for God! God's Son, our Messiah, Jesus, reached across this chasm through His death for us on the cross and is waiting to impart new spiritual life to all who receive His free pardon by faith.

Is this hard to understand? Why are you surprised? It's a miracle! But as a dog named Molly proves, you don't have to fully understand a miracle to be part of one. Will you receive God's redemptive miracle and allow Him to use you to reach across a chasm with His healing, just as He did with Molly and Elisha?

For you who revere my name, the sun of righteousness will rise with healing in its rays (Malachi 4:2).

Consider This:

Has a pet or person ever reached across a physical, mental, or emotional chasm to bring you a healing touch? What happened? How did it help? What did you learn? Is there someone in your life God might want to reach out to through you?

Dogs, Doldrums, and Green Glasses

God Heals Our Perspective

In spite of everything I shall rise again: I will take up my pencil, which I have forsaken in my great discouragement, and I will go on with my drawing.

VINCENT VAN GOGH

Jennell hasn't always made the best choices when it comes to male companionship, but there's one fine fellow who's a keeper for sure. He's the cream in her coffee, the donut to her hole, and a healing light at the end of her emotional tunnel. He takes care of her as best he can, and she does the same for him. She met him on the rebound from a bad relationship, and they've been together ever since. But if you're hearing wedding bells, forget it. One thing Bruno will never be is marriage material, because this golden boy is—a *dog*!

Bruno was God's special gift of joy at a rough point in Jennell's life. She had just gotten out of a bad relationship with someone who had been condescending and emotionally abusive. That situation left her feeling awful. It preyed on her. *How did I let myself get in so deep with him?* she wondered.

Jennell hit bottom. She didn't know how to get out from under the dark cloud of discouragement that was distorting her perspective. Her mom asked her what she wanted, but she didn't know. She had no idea what would fill the void she felt. Mom had a thought. How about a puppy?

That was a prescription Jennell could get used to. But was it God's prescription? She had been asking for His help with her depression. Now she prayed, "Lord, I don't want to seek refuge in a dog. I want to seek refuge in You." She also asked for His wisdom and choice if this was His will. She didn't want to just grab the first dog she saw.

Jennell found Bruno through an ad. He wasn't supposed to be for her. She got there too late and only two of the Boston terrier pups from the litter were left. Tiny Bruno was the runt, and was also spoken for. Even though she was falling in love, it was too late to scoop him up.

Or was it? As she was driving home, bummed that she had missed out, she got a call on her cell phone from the person with the puppies. "She told me she saw how much I loved him and I could come back for him," Jennell said.

Eight-week-old Bruno might have been tiny, but he was mighty when it came to brightening Jennell's world and changing her outlook. "His behavior was so opposite of how I felt," she recalls. "He was just so happy to be happy. He looked at life in a totally different way." Bruno's joy made Jennell look inward and wonder why she had let the ruined relationship defeat her. She felt the devil was in these doldrums and she was not about to let the enemy get the best of her.

Bruno was only too happy to help. "He was so caring and affectionate," she reflected. "He'd come up to me as if to say, 'Let me love you!'" He could be impish and rambunctious too. She'd pretend to be sleeping and he'd take a corner of the bedsheet in his mouth and start pulling it off to make her get up and play with him. He would also tug at her shirt or pants to get her on her feet, and she felt he was pulling her up emotionally as well.

He succeeded—perhaps a little too well for his own doggie liking. Jennell can't spend quite as much time with him these days because she's completing a bachelor's degree in nursing. She was already a practical nurse and this is a further step. Bruno is still her best doggie pal, and she is personally experiencing the truth of Psalm 146:5 (NLT): "But joyful are those who have the God of Israel as their helper, whose hope is in the LORD their God."

God used a puppy to heal Jennell's perspective and turn her gloom to gladness. He used the risen Christ to do this for two downcast disciples on their way to Emmaus (Luke 24:13-33). They didn't recognize Jesus when He first approached them. More significantly, they didn't recognize God's job description for Messiah, even though it was recorded in Scripture. They were bummed because they'd been hoping Jesus was the promised One, but now He'd been crucified. Oh, they'd heard news that the tomb was empty, but that confused them more. They didn't realize Jesus had conquered death; they thought it had conquered Him.

Jesus adjusted their viewpoint by taking them on a guided tour of Messianic prophecy. Later, when He broke bread and handed them some, they recognized Him at last. God's truth transformed their outlook on what had happened, and they rushed back to Jerusalem to share their new perspective with their friends.

One of my favorite illustrations about perspective comes from the book *The Wonderful Wizard of Oz*. Dorothy seeks help from a wizard who rules the Emerald City—so called because everything in it is green. But Dorothy discovers it's all a deception. Everyone who enters the city is told to put on a pair of glasses, and it's the glasses that are green, not the city itself.

Discouragement is a pair of green glasses the devil tries to stick on all of us to drag us down and paralyze our lives. God used a puppy to pull them off Jennell, and Scripture to remove them from the two disciples on their way to Emmaus. He knows how to remove them from us, too, if we will only look to Him and receive His truth, like they did.

Have I not commanded you? Be strong and courageous. Do not be afraid; do not be discouraged, for the LORD your God will be with you wherever you go (Joshua 1:9).

Consider This:

Have you ever felt overwhelmed by discouragement? Who or what got you down? Who or what pulled you up? Are you trapped in green glasses now? What Scriptures might help remove them?

Part II

Doggie Doctor
Knows Best

Addie, Audrey, and Data

A "Dose" of Data

God's Prescriptions Are Perfect

*Dogs are not our whole life, but
they make our lives whole.*

Roger Caras

Addie is a child with multiple health challenges whose most delightful prescription may be a dog named Data. This goldendoodle has been so golden for her and her family that Addie's mom, Sammy, refers to life since getting him as AD (After Doodle).

Life BC (Before Canine) felt at times like scaling a sheer rock wall whose toeholds were shallow, few, and far between. As a baby, Addie had severe GI problems and a multitude of allergies. She was soon diagnosed with a rare lung disease for which there is presently no cure. The cilia or "sweepers" in her lungs don't work right, which means her lungs can't get rid of phlegm and debris normally. She is constantly at risk for lung and ear infections. Addie needs ear tubes till she turns 13, nebulizer treatments daily, and antibiotics every other day just to keep infection at bay.

Addie also has unilateral polymicrogyria (PMG). Part of the frontal lobe of her brain became static in the womb. It just stopped developing. Sammy doesn't know if this is related to her being in a car accident while pregnant, but she does know doctors say it's irreversible. In addition, Addie has been diagnosed with autism and has had some mild seizures.

So what does all that mean for this little girl and her loved ones? Until recently, it meant balancing on the edge of chaos. Addie has zero impulse control, obsessive-compulsive tendencies, and no appropriate boundaries. She's incredibly fast, darts everywhere, and is always ready to wander off. Sammy didn't dare take Addie and her older sister, Audrey, on outings, because Addie was too much of a flight risk. Sammy kept trying to find bright spots of humor while scaling this mountain of challenges. And then, when Addie was not quite four years old, the mountain parted to reveal a pathway—one with four paws and a tail.

Sammy's four-pawed lifesaver came from a nonprofit organization, the amazing 4 Paws for Ability. She had applied to them for a service dog for Addie. They matched Addie with a male goldendoodle named Data. After Sammy and Addie went through a two-week training period with him at the 4 Paws training facility in Xenia, Ohio, they brought Data home to join their family—and he changed their world.

One thing that goes better with Data is Addie's daily nebulizer treatments. As a baby, she used to fight them. These days, her reaction depends on her mood. Data helps by lying next to his girl. She will chatter away to him and pretend she's giving him the treatment, which makes her feel in control.

Data is also a seizure alert dog. He will pre-alert to a seizure by licking and sniffing Addie. If Sammy doesn't pay attention, he'll pace and bump into her till she does. Addie is on anti-seizure medication, but Sammy is grateful that Data can warn her if need be.

Two other talents Data brings to the table are tethering and tracking. It has opened up the world not just for Addie, but also for her sister, Audrey, who is two years older. These days Sammy can take her girls on outings without being petrified that Addie will vanish. She attaches one end of a cord to Data's service dog vest and the other to Addie's belt. That way Addie can't suddenly dart off like she would otherwise be prone to do. They've gone blueberry picking for the first time, and to visit the aquarium. Though Addie does have meltdowns at times, at least she's tethered and they're out of the house, and that's a big step forward.

If Addie ever did manage to bolt, Data could help with that too. The 4 Paws organization taught him to track her, and he's good at it. When Addie and her mom trained with him under 4 Paws supervision, she got to play "hide-and-seek" with her dog, and he proved he could find her.

Though Data is Addie's dog, he has done a world of good for Audrey also. "It's not always easy to be the well child," Sammy told me. "It was very hard for Audrey when we were away in Ohio training with Data, and a big adjustment when we brought him home."

Sammy helped Audrey feel included by giving her the job of brushing Data, feeding him, and putting on his collar. "She lays and cuddles with Data all the time," Sammy said. "She seeks him out and pets and hugs him for her own comfort. He is almost as good for her as he is for Addie."

As for Addie, she loves to boss Data. At times he'll look at Sammy and almost roll his eyes. But he is attentive to Addie and will do what she says when she tells him to come, sit, bark, roll over, and high-five. Addie rewards him with treats she carries around in a special little purse.

Data calms Addie down. Sometimes Sammy comes in to find her daughter on the floor with Data sprawled next to her. She'll be watching TV and involuntarily petting her number one pooch. He also intervenes if she's in a meltdown cycle, some of which can be pretty intense. One way he'll do that is by nuzzling her, but she doesn't like nuzzling all that much, so he has also been taught to bark. This seems to "skip the record" and reset her, startling her out of the meltdown. "Even if it gets her to just start something else, it's good," Sammy told me.

When it comes to a healing influence, Data the dog couldn't be a more perfect prescription for Addie and her family. They didn't need their arms twisted to embrace him, either. But when it comes to God's prescriptions, we humans aren't always quite so quick to receive them or take them as directed.

Two examples come to mind. The first is from 2 Kings 5 and

involves a man stricken with leprosy. This man, Naaman, commanded the armies of the pagan king of Aram. His wife had a Jewish slave girl who urged her to send her husband to a prophet in Israel who could cure him. That prophet was Elisha.

When Naaman finally reached Elisha's door, Elisha sent a messenger to deliver his prescription. "Go, wash yourself seven times in the Jordan, and your flesh will be restored and you will be cleansed" (2 Kings 5:10). But instead of being overjoyed, Naaman stormed off in a fit of rage. How come Elisha didn't come to him personally, call on his God, and heal Naaman on the spot? And since when did the Jordan have superior cleansing powers to the rivers of Naaman's own hometown of Damascus?

Thankfully for Naaman, his servants were wiser than he was. They urged him to follow the prescription rather than scorning it. When he did, he was healed, just like Elisha promised. Naaman proclaimed the greatness of the God of Israel, which is what Elisha wanted, and when he offered the prophet payment, Elisha would not take a penny.

The second less-than-welcome prescription was given by Jesus to a rich young ruler who asked what he must do to have eternal life. Jesus listed several of the Ten Commandments, all of which the young man said he'd been keeping. Then, discerning the underlying problem, Jesus told him, "If you want to be perfect, go, sell what you have and give to the poor, and you will have treasure in heaven; and come, follow Me" (Matthew 19:21 NKJV). But the fellow "went away sorrowful, for he had great possessions" (Matthew 19:22 NKJV).

This man wasn't keeping the first commandment, to love God with all his heart, soul, mind, and strength. He loved his riches more, and couldn't give them up. At the least, Jesus's prescription flagged his ailment for him. And it flags for us that if anything or anyone is first before God, it will affect our spiritual health.

Addie and her family, Naaman, and the rich young ruler all needed a prescription that would be a game changer. All but the rich young ruler took the help they were offered. How about you? The Bible's pages are filled with game-changing prescriptions for health and life. Is a prescription you need waiting for you in its pages?

Do not be wise in your own eyes; fear the LORD and shun evil. This will bring health to your body and nourishment to your bones (Proverbs 3:7-8).

Consider This:

Have you ever suffered from a physical, emotional, or spiritual ailment and gotten a prescription that proved to be a game changer? What was the malady? What were you prescribed? How did it help? Have you been balking at taking a prescription from Scripture?

Her Dogs Walked Her Through Cancer

God's Love Keeps Us Going

*It does not matter how slowly you go
as long as you do not stop.*
Confucius

When Susan started her cancer journey, she never dreamed what a key role her beloved dogs would play in walking her through it. Lilly and Ruby didn't have a clue either. They just did what any loving, loyal canines would—they stuck close to their hurting human and kept her going.

Ruby is a bearded collie Susan got as a 12-week-old puppy. Lilly, a tricolor collie, joined the family when both she and Ruby were two. Susan's four kids had been longing for dogs, but caring for them proved mostly Mom's work. Her husband's first love was cats.

Susan was diagnosed with stage 2 breast cancer in December 2013, when her kids ranged in age from 10 to 20. It came as a huge shock. The tumor was tested and proved to be one with a high recurrence rate, so doctors advised a double mastectomy in January and chemotherapy after that. Susan had a dog-sitter care for her dogs for the first few days after surgery, but it wasn't long before Ruby and Lilly took things into their own paws, flipped the tables, and became caregivers to Susan in their own inimitable doggie way.

"Chemotherapy made me feel like someone poured lead into my body," Susan told me. "Every bit of my energy was drained." Her dogs knew something was wrong and would not leave her side. They followed Susan everywhere, as if stuck to her with Velcro. When she was lying on the couch, Lilly would put her head on the sofa and stare. Ruby had slept by Susan's feet at night; now she moved up and slept by Susan's head.

Susan credits her dogs with getting her up and moving when she would have much preferred to vegetate. "I would not have gotten up as soon," she told me. But the dogs had been used to long walks when she was healthy, and she felt like she had to try to take them out because they were depending on her. A nurse by profession, she knew the longer she stayed down, the weaker she'd get. She knew inactivity could cause a buildup of fluid and mucus in the lungs. She knew the risk of blood clots and pneumonia was higher if she just lay around. But what she knew would not have been enough to pull her to her feet.

"You feel so sick that you want to give up. You don't care anymore," Susan said. But she cared about Ruby and Lilly, and they cared about her. Some patients take sleeping pills and antidepressants in her situation. Not Susan. Her two four-pawed "person-sitters" kept her focused and happy. They gave her an emotional "up" and a purpose for getting out of bed in the morning, just in how they connected to her with their eyes. Her family had to go to school and work, but the dogs were with her constantly, so she never felt alone. Her furry buddies provided much-needed companionship and were also a living alarm system, barking if anyone approached the house.

It was a bitterly cold winter where Susan lives in Wisconsin, and no one went out much. But the dogs did get her out a little. They adjusted their pace to hers. They walked more slowly. They let Susan build up gradually. First she walked them half a block, then a full block, and later a loop around the neighborhood as she got stronger and the weather got warmer. Susan began to feel better, even as her bond with her devoted dogs deepened.

Susan's last chemotherapy treatment was June 24, 2014. She's had a couple of other health blips since, but she's made it through. In the midst of it, she's built up to walking the dogs three times a day, and dogs and human all improved their fitness levels. At this point she is cancer-free and has an 85 percent chance of staying that way. She says cancer has changed her for the better. She's more patient now. Looks and possessions matter less, and her friendships, both human and canine, while always precious to her, matter more than ever. She is eternally grateful to Ruby and Lilly for the healing they've brought her, and feels blessed to have them beside her as she walks toward her future.

Thinking of how Susan's dogs walked beside her through a dark time in her life reminds me of God's desire to do the same for us. This is beautifully put by one of the most famous passages in Scripture, Psalm 23 (TLB).

> Because the Lord is my Shepherd, I have everything I need! He lets me rest in the meadow grass and leads me beside the quiet streams. He gives me new strength. He helps me do what honors him the most. Even when walking through the dark valley of death I will not be afraid, for you are close beside me, guarding, guiding all the way. You provide delicious food for me in the presence of my enemies. You have welcomed me as your guest; blessings overflow! Your goodness and unfailing kindness shall be with me all of my life, and afterwards I will live with you forever in your home.

Susan's dogs stayed close to their human. Not only is God with us; He puts His Spirit within us if we've given our lives to Him. Susan's dogs gave her strength to boost her physical and emotional health. God empowers us to lead spiritually healthy lives. Susan's dogs walked her through grueling treatment. God promises to walk us through death itself.

I decided to look at what a famous commentator, Charles H. Spurgeon, had to say about Psalm 23. Two of his observations on verse 4 leaped out at me. The King James Version translates the first part of this verse, "Yea, though I walk through the valley of the shadow of death, I will fear no evil: for thou art with me." Spurgeon points out that if we have put our faith in Jesus, physical death is only a shadow, and a shadow can't harm us. Moreover we don't remain in this valley of death's shadow; we walk *through* it to a wondrous eternity with God.

What better future could you walk toward than that?

For you have delivered me from death and my feet from stumbling, that I may walk before God in the light of life (Psalm 56:13).

Consider This:

Have you ever had a pet or human walk you through a dark time? How did they help? What did it mean to you? How has God walked with you? How might you walk with someone else?

Kiki's Doggie Diagnostics
Our Great Physician Knows Us Inside Out

*Let the young know they will never find a more inter-
esting, more instructive book than the patient himself.*

GIORGIO BAGLIVI

Kiki is a seizure alert dog who has far exceeded expectations. She has
proved to be something of a doggie Sherlock Holmes. She is a medical
early warning system not only for her special charge, Savanna, but for
the child's whole family as well.

Savanna's mom, Stephanie, will never forget her daughter's first
seizure. Savanna was only two months old. Hubby J.D. was in the
military and had been deployed in Iraq since before the baby's birth.
Stephanie was home alone with Savanna and her older brother, Jake.
She was walking past her daughter's room and got a bad feeling. She
rushed to her baby and saw that her eyes were open and she wasn't
breathing.

Savanna lived through this grand mal episode and was diagnosed
with epilepsy. She was put on medication. Stephanie had a hard time
sleeping and couldn't be away from her child. She doesn't know what
she would have done if not for her own mom's support. Thankfully, her
husband made it home when Savanna was five months of age and it

seemed like Savanna's medication was working. After two years seemingly seizure-free on the meds, the doctor weaned Savanna off them. He told Stephanie if her daughter could go two more years without having a seizure, her risk of recurrence was minimal. Another year and a half passed. The seizures returned.

"They came back angry," Stephanie told me. At the worst point, Savanna sometimes had three a day. Severity varied, but it was a tough, scary time. Stephanie remembered hearing years earlier that dogs were being trained to help kids like Savanna. She did some research and applied to several organizations for a service dog, and 4 Paws for Ability said yes.

This organization is nonprofit, but children's families are asked to fund-raise for the 4 Paws mission and help raise a target amount to qualify for a free service dog. Stephanie was doing this when a gift came out of nowhere. She had shared Savanna's story on the 4 Paws Make A Wish page. An angel donor whose own child had epilepsy and wanted to help a veteran's family gave the balance of what was needed to meet the goal.

Kiki is a beautiful yellow Labrador retriever who has been a huge blessing to her humans, sometimes in unexpected ways. She has done all she was trained to do, and more. Kiki knows basic obedience and also learned how to open doors and help Savanna keep her balance. That's important because the seizures and some seizure medications may cause dizziness. Some medications may also have emotional side effects. Kiki has been taught "behavior disruption." She will nuzzle Savanna on command, which helps calm her if she is having a meltdown.

But Kiki's biggest job is pre-alerting before a seizure happens. Kiki will obsessively lick Savanna's ears, nose, mouth, and especially the palms of her hands and her feet. She will also try to get the parents' attention. Kiki's actions make Savanna giggle and she thinks it's fun, but the adults realize what this means and can prepare to keep Savanna safe when the seizure happens.

Most often, Kiki pre-alerts about three hours before a seizure occurs. She also helps Savanna's parents pick up on seizures that occur at night, seizures they may have been missing before.

Thanks to this beloved medical detective with paws, Savanna's neurologist has been able to fine-tune her treatment. The child's seizures have markedly decreased. "We could have gone many years without fully knowing what was going on. Kiki made all the difference," Stephanie said.

Kiki adores her little girl and is something of a canine nanny. "She's so worried about where Savanna is. She's right on her heels all the time," Stephanie told me. But this precious dog isn't just concerned about Savanna. She looks out for the rest of the family too.

One example of this involved Savanna's older brother, Jake. When the nine-year-old complained of pain one day, his mom might not have realized it was as serious as it was. But Kiki let her know by relentlessly licking Jake and nudging her that something more concerning was up. She was out the door with Jake in half an hour headed for the ER. It turned out Jake had kidney stones.

Proving she's not just concerned about the kids in the family, Kiki also pre-alerted with hubby J.D. on a particular evening. Later that night he was taken to the hospital with chest pains. They admitted him and diagnosed early onset heart disease.

But perhaps the most dramatic pre-alerting Kiki did was with Stephanie herself. She was working with the school system to mainstream Savanna in a regular classroom and wanted Kiki to pre-alert there as well. Because Kiki needed an adult handler, Stephanie had been going to school with her daughter and the dog. So when Kiki started licking Stephanie's palms and abdomen, she wasn't concerned. She just thought perhaps Kiki was getting too attached to her. She realized differently two weeks later when shortness of breath and lots of chest pain landed her in the ER. Doctors found blood clots in both her lungs. Stephanie suffers from a hereditary blood disorder and had been on a blood thinner, but clearly it wasn't working. Doctors thought the clots came from her pelvis, which might explain Kiki's interest in her abdomen.

Needless to say, these days Kiki's family takes her concerns seriously. They also love this dog to pieces. They never had pups before, but now they can't imagine life without her. Kiki even won over Stephanie's mom, who was not a dog person. "We have this huge sense of togetherness," Stephanie said. "Kiki makes life better. She gets this look on her face, like she's telling me it will all be okay. I feel safer because I know she's doing her job."

Kiki has also become part of Stephanie's wonderful church family. "They adore Kiki. She gets under the pews and sleeps. She will walk up to our pastor, plop on his feet, and refuse to move until he pets her. She's such a big part of every aspect of our life."

As I thought of Kiki and her doggie diagnostics, I began to ponder the infinitely deeper diagnostic wisdom of our Great Physician, God. He knows us inside out, physically and spiritually. He knows our ills and what most needs attention. Scripture has many examples, but the one that comes to mind is the story of Jesus healing the paralytic (Luke 5:17-26).

Jesus was in Capernaum. A huge crowd had gathered at the house where he was teaching. Among them were four men on a mission. They had brought a paralyzed friend for healing, but they couldn't get him through the crowd to put him before Jesus. They did not give up, however. They climbed up on the roof with their pal, removed some tiles, and lowered him down through the opening to the Lord.

According to Luke 5:20, "When Jesus saw their faith, he said, 'Friend, your sins are forgiven.'"

This man's paralysis was visible for all to see. His spiritual ills were not. Jesus alerted to his spiritual state and dealt with it. In fact, He saw fit to address it first. Sin must be dealt with, because the more it is left unchecked, the more damage it is apt to cause.

Jesus saw something else others didn't. He saw the hearts of the religious leaders in the room. They were suffering from unbelief. They thought He had committed blasphemy, because only God could forgive sins, right? And He wasn't God…or *was* He? Jesus alerted to their error by asking, "Why do you question this in your hearts? Is it easier to say 'Your sins are forgiven,' or 'Stand up and walk'? So I will prove to you that the Son of Man has the authority on earth to forgive sins" (Luke 5:22-24 NLT). He proceeded to heal the man physically, to the shock and awe of all present, and the glory of God!

Kiki the dog can alert her humans that something is wrong and needs healing, but she can't make them well. God can both diagnose and heal. Will you ask Him to guide you to spiritual health?

Search me, God, and know my heart; test me and know my anxious thoughts. See if there is any offensive way in me, and lead me in the way everlasting (Psalm 139:23-24).

Consider This:

Has God or a fellow believer ever alerted you to a spiritual malady in your life that needed healing? Were you aware of it? Did you heed the warning? What was the result? Do you need to ask God to search your heart right now?

Dr. Fred and the Incredible, Unexpected, Not Very Wonderful but Ultimately Lifesaving Diagnosis

God Can Bring Gain from Pain

*Pain insists upon being attended to. God whispers to us
in our pleasures, speaks in our consciences, but shouts in
our pains. It is his megaphone to rouse a deaf world.*
C.S. LEWIS

Dr. Fred didn't practice medicine. He offered tips on real estate and foods you shouldn't feed your canine. But in a miraculous example of God's provision, his last act on earth was to aid in making a lifesaving diagnosis. That would have been amazing enough under any circumstances, but consider this: Dr. Fred was a dog.

The person Fred helped save was his beloved human mom, Jenean. She and her husband, Gary, adopted him from an animal shelter when the black Labrador was about two years old. His first healing mission in her life was to brighten her day. "I think animals are God's way of adding a healing touch to people's lives," she told me. She was a Realtor who worked a lot from her home office and found real estate something of a lonely job at times.

It could be stressful too. "Buying a home is the largest expense people may have in their lifetime, and as their Realtor, you're in charge of helping them through it," she reflected. Fred was a funny dog and he made her laugh, which doctors agree is good medicine in all kinds of ways. And in short order, Fred became a part of the business and was bringing a smile to her clients as well.

Jenean wrote a monthly newsletter and Fred had his own column, "Fred's Corner"—ghosted by her, of course. He was allowed to say things Jenean couldn't. She'd also dress Fred in funny outfits and take photos. A new picture graced the newsletter every month. In one photo he was dressed in a lab coat (hey, he was a LABrador). For that newsletter, "Dr. Fred" offered tips about "What Dogs Shouldn't Eat." But Fred's finest medical moment was yet to come.

Fred lived to the ripe old age (for a Lab) of 14. Jenean knew for about a month that the end was coming. He'd stopped eating and was getting weaker. On one particular day, she realized it was time. She made an appointment to take him to the vet when her husband got home from work. She was distraught with sadness, and cried all day.

Crying that long and that hard took its toll. Without warning, she was jolted by a pain in her chest. She grabbed herself and felt something like a rock in her breast. She had never felt that before. It didn't seem like a cyst. Somehow, in her heart, she knew she had cancer.

Jenean had had a mammogram not long before this happened. It showed nothing. The pain she felt that day subsided and never returned. She believes it was brought on by the intensity of her sobbing. If not for her grief over Fred, she's not sure how long it might have taken to find this lump. Saving her life was his last gift to her.

Jenean and Gary put Fred down. The next day, she saw her doctor. Tests done a couple of weeks later revealed she had an invasive, aggressive, fast-growing cancer. In that small amount of time, the lump got 50 percent larger. Chemo was started immediately, followed in 12 weeks by a mastectomy, then more chemo when some stray cancer cells were discovered.

Jenean saw Fred as God's provision to reveal the cancer. She continued to see God's loving care for her throughout her treatment. Jenean had had a great six months financially right before the diagnosis, so there were extra funds while she couldn't work. A friend from a small group she and Gary were in said she felt God tapped her on the shoulder and asked her to take Jenean to every single doctor's appointment— and she did! And there was the matter of a health complication she suffered that got resolved in an amazing way.

Jenean developed what she described as an "acquired colitis" due to a bacterium called C. diff that got into her system while she was in the hospital. She had to take extremely expensive medicine specially compounded at her pharmacy, and her case was so severe that the medicine did not cure her; it just kept her symptoms at bay. There was a procedure being used successfully to treat this in certain other countries, but it had not been approved in the United States, and extremely tight FDA restrictions had been placed on its use. Jenean's specialist was keeping close watch on developments in this area, and when the FDA eased these restrictions and temporarily authorized the procedure for cases like hers on an experimental basis, he spotted it right away. Incredibly, Michelle, the compounder at her pharmacy, volunteered to be her donor for the procedure. Jenean was able to have it done and was cured in one day.

But perhaps most heart-grabbing of all is how God used her illness to deepen her bond with a treasured friend who was also battling cancer. Their common struggle opened the door for Jenean to share God's love more fully, and it meant the world to her!

Thankfully, Jenean herself has now been declared cancer-free. Her most recent test results look great. Her blood and body show no traces that she ever had a malignancy. She and Gary have a new dog in their lives—a silver Labrador named Buck. Jenean tells me Buck has taken up Fred's mantle by "writing" his own "Buck's Corner" in her real estate newsletter. She and her husband are looking forward to the laughs and healing touches he will bring them, hopefully for many years to come.

When I think of how God used pain to bring healing in Jenean's life, I'm reminded of the apostle Paul. This mighty messenger of the gospel suffered untold hardships and agony sharing God's healing love and forgiveness with his world. And at times he was forced to communicate painful truth to others for the sake of their spiritual health. One such incident is recorded in 2 Corinthians 7:8-10 (MSG). Paul writes,

> I know I distressed you greatly with my letter. Although I felt awful at the time, I don't feel at all bad now that I see how it turned out. The letter upset you, but only for a while. Now I'm glad—not that you were upset, but that you were jarred into turning things around. You let the distress bring you to God, not drive you from him. The result was all gain, no loss. Distress that drives us to God does that. It turns us around. It gets us back in the way of salvation. We never regret that kind of pain. But those who let distress drive them away from God are full of regrets, end up on a deathbed of regrets.

Jenean responded positively to pain and allowed God to use it for healing in her own and others' lives. Paul the apostle did the same. What will you choose?

Before I was afflicted I went astray, but now I obey your word (Psalm 119:67).

Consider This:

Has God ever used your own or someone else's pain for gain in your life or theirs? What happened? What did you learn? Are you suffering physical or emotional pain right now that might be God's wake-up call?

The Dog That Empowered a Peanut

Hope Is Healing

Hope is the thing with feathers
That perches in the soul,
And sings the tune without the words,
And never stops at all.

EMILY DICKINSON

Barbie is a wonderful young woman who began life as a Peanut. At least, that was her nickname, and for good reason. She was born when her mother was only 26 and a half weeks pregnant and weighed not quite two pounds. She survived, but was left with spastic cerebral palsy. In her words, "My brain and body don't agree with each other very much."

One big challenge was mobility. Barbie used a scooter or a walker, but she needed someone's help to do it. In addition to difficulty walking, she had balance issues and was in danger of falling. She also had trouble doing the small things most of us take for granted, such as opening doors, picking up the phone, or retrieving something she dropped.

No matter. Barbie was an overcomer. Her heart was bigger than her challenges. She longed to do more for herself and someday hold a full- or part-time job. She had aids to help her in high school, but in tech school, finding the right person to assist her got harder. And she sometimes had to be home alone because her mom worked. She saw she needed a different solution to stay safe and reach for her dreams— a helper with four paws instead of two feet.

Barbie contacted 4 Paws for Ability. They agreed to match her with a dog. Recipients and their families are asked to help raise a target amount for the 4 Paws mission to qualify for a free service dog. When Barbie's efforts stalled, she got a jump-start from an unexpected source. She was with her mom at a flea market when a stranger asked what she wanted for Christmas. "A service dog," she replied. That stranger turned out to be a reporter. Barbie was interviewed on TV and even more money came in than she needed.

Barbie had to pick up her Christmas present, but she didn't mind at all. In June 2009 she traveled not to the North Pole but to the 4 Paws training facility in Xenia, Ohio. There she met and trained with Maestro, a male golden retriever who changed her life.

"I don't feel like I burden people as much now that I have Maestro," she told me. "If I need help he's always around." He'll grab the phone when it rings and take it to her, or fetch it on command. He also knows how to open and close the fridge and put things in the trash. When they're out he pushes the buttons that open automatic doors. With the help of a special device, Maestro can also tug a door open far enough that Barbie can do the rest.

When she first got Maestro, Barbie felt a bit intimidated. She was scared to use him as an aid to mobility. But at a later date, one of her therapists pointed out that moving more might keep her in better health. She decided to go for it, and sent Maestro back for this extra mobility balance training. Now, with the help of a special harness positioned between his head and shoulders, he helps Barbie walk. She holds onto the handle and he steadies her. He can also tell if she's going to stumble or fall. If it's a stumble, he'll stop in his tracks. If he senses she's headed for a fall, he will cross in front of her so she can brace herself against him. Now and then she does fall, and she'll use him to help pull herself back up.

Thanks to Maestro, Barbie has a whole new level of confidence and independence, and she's so happy she does. She can get around without a wheelchair or a walker, though she still uses them from time to time. With her service dog by her side, she can go to the park or store without another human by her side. She can step up and down curbs without human help. If she's in a public place, she can navigate the bathroom or the cafeteria. And if she's home alone she doesn't need to worry, because her four-pawed hero is there to help.

In short, Maestro is Barbie's bundle of hope wrapped in fur. He has helped her conquer obstacles she never thought she could. He has opened the eyes of her heart to the fuller life she can have with her doggie helper by her side. Thinking about this, I was reminded of a marvelous Old Testament story about healing hope from God (2 Kings 6:8-22).

The man who needed this healing hope was the servant of the Jewish prophet Elisha. This poor servant thought he and his master were doomed. Aram was at war with Israel, and Elisha had been giving the Israelite king intel on the movement of the enemy army. The king of Aram had learned that Elisha was in the city of Dothan and sent his forces to surround it. Elisha's servant woke up in the morning, saw this seemingly insurmountable obstacle of an army, and was terrified.

Elisha wasn't scared at all. He knew he had God by his side, he trusted the Lord, and he saw what his servant didn't. He asked God to make his servant see too. "Then the LORD opened the servant's eyes, and he looked and saw the hills full of horses and chariots of fire all around Elisha" (2 Kings 6:17).

God helped Elisha see a lot more than fiery chariots and horses. Elisha saw how to deal with his enemies in a most unexpected way. He asked God to strike the enemy army blind. Then he tricked them and led them into a trap, after which their sight was restored. Rather than kill them, he advised the Israelite king to throw them a feast. Then that army was released to return to the king of Aram and open *his* eyes to the greatness of the God of Israel. Hostilities stopped.

Barbie's dog, Maestro, has given her hope and new ways to see the future. Hoping in God will change your perspective too. Will you let Him open your eyes, as He did for Elisha's servant?

Be strong and take heart, all you who hope in the LORD (Psalm 31:24).

Consider This:

Have any pets or people given you hope in the midst of despair? What obstacles were you facing? How did they help? How has God been a source of healing hope and new perspective?

Nate's Chevy Gate
God Is Our Gate to Healing

Still round the corner there may wait,
A new road or a secret gate.
J.R.R. TOLKIEN

Nate has a Chevy that helps him stay safe and get where he needs to go. But his Chevy isn't a car; it's a golden retriever. Chevy is Nate's beloved service dog, and the gate through which Nate can enter into a fuller, richer life.

Ten-year-old Nate was born with Down syndrome, a genetic disorder that results in mental and developmental challenges. In some cases it may trigger other health problems too. Nate's mom, Tania, a registered nurse, told me one in 90 children with Down syndrome also gets leukemia. Nate is one of those.

Nate's issues started with a growth in his windpipe. Doctors had to insert a tube to help him breathe. At first they thought it was due to a virus, but when it didn't go away, they had to remove the growth surgically. Six months later, they took out the tube. The leukemia diagnosis came a week afterward.

A bumpy three and a half years of chemotherapy followed. Since he had a small airway, Nate was more prone to respiratory infections. He was in and out of the hospital a lot. Thankfully, he is now in remission, but he has to go for blood draws every couple of months.

Due to Nate's challenges, his parents decided their only child needed a buddy. Nate had always loved dogs. Tania and her husband, Ken, had friends whose children had service dogs. They hoped maybe one could help Nate too.

The first organization they contacted turned Nate down. Then they reached out to 4 Paws for Ability. This nonprofit focuses on providing service dogs for veterans and children with special needs. Nate was approved and paired with his beloved Chevy, and he and his family went through two weeks of training with their new furry family member at the 4 Paws training facility in Xenia, Ohio.

Chevy is a gate for Nate in a variety of ways. Children with Down syndrome are prone to wander off. Nate did this one night during training, wandering out of his hotel room in the wee hours and knocking on a stranger's door. Fortunately, the gentleman who answered had worked with kids with special needs, recognized the situation, and alerted the front desk.

Now, however, Nate has his Chevy gate to help keep him safe. Chevy has been trained in tracking. If Nate goes AWOL, his dog can pick up his trail. One day Nate walked out of his garage and down the block. A neighbor spotted him and then saw Chevy fly around the corner. No one knows if the pair got out together, but Tania is grateful they have a four-pawed detective who can help find their son if the need should ever arise.

Chevy is also a gate to comfort. Nate doesn't like the blood draws he has to submit to periodically. Chevy always goes with him, and if Nate is hurting or crying, Chevy kisses him, which calms Nate immediately. Chevy will only kiss Nate, no one else. At home, Chevy rushes to his boy if he hears Nate sounding upset.

But best of all, Chevy is Nate's gate to a richer, fuller life. One thing he's done is encourage Nate's verbal development. Kids with Down syndrome can struggle with this, Tania told me. That's because they have low muscle tone and poor motor planning. "To speak, our brain has to tell our muscles what to do," she explained. Nate may have had further speech delays because of the breathing tube and side effects of certain chemo medications. But he had an explosion of speech during his two weeks of dog training in Ohio. It may be that his desire to teach Chevy verbal commands helped trigger his spurt.

Nate goes to school in a suburb of Chicago and is mainstreamed in a regular classroom. Chevy goes too, and is handled by Nate's instructional assistant. Nate seems more grounded with Chevy around. He does better with paying attention and he seems to find Chevy a comforting presence.

Chevy is supposed to be a social interaction tool and almost all the kids at school love him. Even when children are afraid of the dog, they usually get over it. Tania noticed that one autistic little boy on Nate's bus seemed terrified of Chevy. But that same child warmed up and invited both Nate and his dog to his birthday celebration. Chevy was the hit of the party.

Nate scores highest in social skills and memory. But due to his motor challenges, he can't play most sports. Here, too, Chevy has been a gate by drawing Nate into a sport he and his dog can have a blast competing in together.

That sport is dock diving, also known as dock jumping, and Chevy loves it. He just about loses his mind when he gets to participate. Nate wears superhero shirts to the meets and his job is to throw a toy off a dock into a body of water and release his dog. Chevy must leap off the dock and retrieve the item. Dogs are scored on how high or how far they jump.

Taking part in dock diving has opened all kinds of new worlds for Nate. Others in the sport are nice to him and engage him. Kids with Down syndrome are easily overstimulated and tend to retreat when that happens, but being at the competitions has helped Nate learn to tolerate that kind of environment better.

"We would never be able to be where we are today with Nate if we hadn't gotten a service dog," Tania concluded. "Chevy is so well trained and so in tune with him. I couldn't be with Nate all the time like Chevy is, and it has made such a difference!"

As I pondered Chevy as Nate's gate, it made me think of Jesus as the gate of His sheep. In John 10:7-10 Jesus says,

> Very truly I tell you, I am the gate for the sheep. All who have come before me are thieves and robbers, but the sheep have not listened to them. I am the gate; whoever enters through me will be saved. They will come in and go out, and find pasture. The thief comes only to steal and kill and destroy; I have come that they may have life, and have it to the full.

There was an actual Sheep Gate in Jerusalem, and sheep passed through this gate on their way to be sacrificed at the temple. In John 1:29, John the Baptist says of Jesus, "Look, the Lamb of God, who takes away the sin of the world!" Jesus also says in John 14:6, "I am the way and the truth and the life. No one comes to the Father except through me."

Chevy has been vital to Nate's healing, and Jesus is vital to ours. None of us could purchase God's forgiveness or in any way earn it. Jesus is both our gate to the Father and the Good Shepherd who nurtures us on our spiritual journey. That same Good Shepherd goes in search of us if we wander away, just like Chevy does for Nate.

Nate embraced Chevy and joyfully entered the gate to healing that he provided. Jesus the gate is open to all who will come. Have you entered in?

Small is the gate and narrow the road that leads to life, and only a few find it (Matthew 7:14).

Consider This:

Have any people or pets been a gate to healing for you? In what way? How is Jesus your gate to spiritual healing and growth?

The Dog at the End of Their Rope
God's Healing Gifts Amaze

God's gifts put man's best dreams to shame.
Elizabeth Barrett Browning

Maggie and her family were at their wits' end, but no place is too dark or hopeless for God to enter. He met them there with the healing gift they needed. That gift was Kermit, who is no frog despite his name. He is a bloodhound/Labrador retriever mix who doubles as son Danny's service dog and the whole family's canine knight in shining armor.

Kermit was chosen and trained by the nonprofit 4 Paws for Ability, an organization willing to tackle tough cases. Danny was definitely one of those! He has autism, an impulse control disorder, and intractable epilepsy. When the six-footer has a seizure he can fall like a tree. Over the course of his life he has broken his nose, fractured many teeth, and suffered numerous concussions. The constant challenge has been how to keep him safe, and Kermit has made all the difference.

Danny may have had seizures from birth, but the first one his parents know about was a grand mal seizure at five months of age. He was diagnosed with autistic tendencies at age two. Growing up, he was so hyper that his school took his desk and bolted it to a board. Mom Maggie described it as "ADD times a thousand." He was also prone to wander off and knew no fear—when he was little, he got fished out of a lake three times.

In his early twenties, Danny was having a grand mal seizure every nine to ten days. He also had other smaller partial seizures as well. After a grand mal episode, it would be four or five hours before he could stand up. He even had a special device, which is like a pacemaker for the brain, implanted under one armpit. It helped some, but there were still huge issues no one could deal with.

Kermit was the missing puzzle piece that proved to be a game changer. Even fund-raising was a miracle. The 4 Paws organization asks that recipients and their families help raise a target amount toward the cost of a dog's training and placement to qualify for a free service dog. When Maggie and her family fund-raised, the money poured in and they got almost twice their goal amount, which meant someone else could be helped with the excess.

Kermit joined the family and has been the greatest tool by far for Danny's seizure control and safety. But first, he and his humans had to fine-tune their communication. Maggie recalls one incident three months after Kermit arrived. A sitter was watching Danny while she was out. The sitter called and said Kermit was going ballistic. He'd ripped up some plants and she feared he might have eaten something poisonous. Maggie raced home, and by the time she got there, Danny had had a seizure. Kermit hadn't been sick at all; he was doing his job. The sitter had been heading out the door to the store with Danny in tow, and Kermit sensed a seizure was coming and was trying to alert her.

Kermit's advance warning of Danny's seizures has helped his loved ones keep Danny safer. He hasn't wound up in the ER for over four years. These alerts have also been key in enabling his family and doctors to come up with some promising seizure reduction strategies over time. When I interviewed Danny's mom for this story, he had recently gone from one grand mal seizure every nine or ten days to two in six weeks. It was summer, a time when his seizures would normally increase, and instead, he'd had fewer than ever before.

Kermit helps with Danny in other ways too. He will herd Danny, lie on his feet, or block the door to keep his charge from wandering off. Kermit also chills Danny out when he gets agitated. "He reads Danny really well," Maggie told me. "He'll go into Danny's room even if Danny is having a bad day and slamming things around." Kermit also tags along on Danny's doctor appointments, which can be a nightmare if the dog isn't there.

As I've thought of the role Kermit plays in Danny's care, it seems that he is like the key piece in a puzzle. Fitting him in brings the other puzzle pieces together in a whole new way. Fitting Jesus the Messiah into God's redemptive puzzle does the same with respect to our spiritual health.

The Bible tells us we humans are at our wits' end when it comes to sin. We have no lasting way to deal with it. But God met us at the end of our rope with the healing gift we needed—our Messiah and Savior, Jesus Christ. Jesus has done double duty as both the once-for-all sacrifice that paid for our sins forever and our High Priest who constantly intercedes for us with the Father. However, God has had to work with us to fine-tune our understanding of our spiritual need and His solution to it.

This was true even for Nicodemus, a renowned first-century Jewish religious leader. He came to Jesus under cover of darkness because he realized this controversial Teacher was someone special. But when Jesus told him he had to be born again to see God's kingdom, Nicodemus was mystified. "'What do you mean?' exclaimed Nicodemus. 'How can an old man go back into his mother's womb and be born again?' Jesus replied, 'I assure you, no one can enter the Kingdom of God without being born of water and the Spirit. Humans can reproduce only human life, but the Holy Spirit gives birth to spiritual life'" (John 3:4-6 NLT).

Nicodemus didn't get it then, but in time he came to understand that Jesus was the pivotal puzzle piece in God's plan of redemption. He put his faith in his Messiah, was born again spiritually, and received the free gift of God's forgiveness and eternal life. That same free gift is waiting for you at the end of your spiritual rope. Have you let God make you whole?

Now he has made all of this plain to us by the appear-ing of Christ Jesus, our Savior. He broke the power of death and illuminated the way to life and immortality through the Good News (2 Timothy 1:10 NLT).

Consider This:

Have you ever had someone give you a healing gift when you were at the end of your rope? What was the gift? Who gave it? How did it help? How can you do this for someone else? How has God met you when you were at your wits' end?

Lifeline in Fur
God's Warnings Are Healing

A danger foreseen is half avoided.
PROVERB

For most people, surviving college means passing tests, getting by on less rest, and maybe finding the right financial aid package. But for Makenzie, the stakes are much higher. She has a health issue that could cause her to slip into a coma in her sleep. That's why her service dog, Bentley, is literally a lifeline in fur.

Makenzie was diagnosed with type 1 diabetes at age seven. She'd been lethargic and irritable, and when it persisted, her parents got concerned. They took her to the doctor and her blood sugar level told the story. It was off-the-charts high. Doctors suspected it had been going on for a while. If it had kept on much longer, she might not have lived.

Normally, blood sugar is regulated by the hormone insulin, which is made by islet cells in the pancreas. In most cases of type 1 diabetes, the immune system misfires. It goes haywire and attacks these cells by mistake, destroying or severely damaging the body's insulin-making capability. Fortunately, people with this disease can live active, full lives with proper medical management. But it takes constant vigilance and can be tougher for some than for others.

Makenzie's diagnosis rocked her world. From that moment, her life changed. Her time in the hospital was just the beginning. She turned out to have a trickier case, because her pancreas still had some insulin-producing capability. It could, and would, start up without warning, dumping spurts of insulin into her body and causing crazy blood sugar lows that came on fast. If this wasn't corrected quickly, Makenzie could become confused and slip into a diabetic coma. Frequent blood sugar checks were essential, including at night, because if she "went low" in her sleep, she might not wake up.

Makenzie's parents were always supportive of her, just as they were with her siblings. They didn't want diabetes to hold her back. She came to view it more as a challenge than a burden. When facing some new hurdle, her attitude was, "You folks just have a seat and watch me make this happen." Still, Makenzie couldn't do some things, like sleep over at a friend's or spend a week away at camp, because no one knew how to care for her like her parents did. Her dad got up three times a night, every night, throughout her childhood and high school years, to check his sleeping daughter's blood sugar and make sure she was okay.

As the time for college drew nearer, Makenzie longed to go away to school. But how would she manage without Dad to watch over her? How could she break the health chains that bound her and still stay safe? A ray of hope came through a friend with a service dog. His mom told her dogs had been trained to alert to low and high blood sugar levels. While such dogs were not a substitute for precautions the doctor recommended, they could provide an additional layer of protection. Could such a dog be the key that unlocked Makenzie's future?

Most diabetic alert dogs are professionally trained. But Makenzie had grown up on a cattle ranch. She loved animals and already had some dog training mojo. She decided to look into choosing and training her own service dog. After researching training methods, she launched a dog search and found a breeder with a tricolored Australian shepherd pup that looked promising indeed.

Baby Bentley pawed her way into Makenzie's heart and life at 12 weeks of age. Makenzie kept her close and worked with her constantly. Bentley needed to learn her human's scent, and how it changed when

Makenzie was in blood sugar trouble. And she had to alert that something was wrong. Bentley was curious and also extremely loving, which made her a great candidate for the task at hand. But would she catch on? Would the training work?

Bentley provided the answer when she was eight or nine months old. Makenzie was ill and lying on the couch. Bentley sat on top of her and whimpered. Makenzie thought her dog was asking to go potty and got up to let her out, but Bentley wouldn't budge. When Makenzie sprawled back on the couch, Bentley began pawing at her. Makenzie's mom came into the room, saw what the dog was doing, and told her daughter she needed to test. What if Bentley was trying to tell her that her blood sugar had dropped?

Testing confirmed that this was exactly what Bentley was doing. "I praised her like crazy," she told me. "I was so excited!" Once she got her blood sugar back up, Bentley calmed down.

Bentley continued to hone her skills as she and her human headed to college. She acts differently when something is amiss. She'll whimper constantly, paw at Makenzie, and get right in her face, as if to say, "Listen to me! You're not right! You need to fix this!" Last year when Makenzie was home for Christmas, Bentley woke her up one night by jumping on her and going crazy. When Makenzie tested, her blood sugar was 45. The bottom of the normal range for fasting blood sugar is 70.

These days Bentley also alerts to significant blood sugar drops that don't go below the normal range. That's important, since it clues Makenzie that her levels are less stable. She then knows to test more often.

Dog mom Makenzie bursts with pride at how well-behaved her fur child is. Bentley flips a behavioral switch when her service dog vest goes on. She'll walk quietly beside her human and sit when Makenzie stops. She parks herself beneath Makenzie's desk in class, or under the table in a restaurant. Most people don't even notice she's there.

But Bentley has another side too. When her vest is off and she's chilling with her human at home, she's a goofy little clown. She's affectionate and playful, and delights to jump on Makenzie and lick her. Makenzie loves it too!

Bentley's training is ongoing. Makenzie's low blood sugar fix of choice is a portion-sized container of apple juice. She's trying to teach Bentley to open the fridge and fetch one for her. And Bentley isn't as consistent in alerting to high blood sugar, though she picks up on it some of the time. This isn't quite as critical though, since Makenzie tests herself five to seven times a day and the danger doesn't build as rapidly.

A college sophomore as of this writing, Makenzie is majoring in kinesiology and working part-time as a personal trainer. One day she hopes to work with kids who, like her, have type 1 diabetes, helping them to stay fit and eat right. She views Bentley as a partner in that dream and feels blessed by how much safer and more peaceful she feels with her beloved best doggie pal by her side.

Bentley is an early warning system in fur. God gives us early warning systems too. In this fallen world, it's a tricky business to keep our spiritual health in balance. His Word can alert us that our spiritual blood sugar is going low and paw at us to drink the apple juice of repentance. In Psalm 19:9,11 (NLT) we read, "The laws of the LORD are true; each one is fair…They are a warning to your servant, a great reward for those who obey them." Hebrews 4:12 spotlights this further: "For the word of God is alive and active. Sharper than any double-edged sword, it penetrates even to dividing soul and spirit, joints and marrow; it judges the thoughts and attitudes of the heart."

God's Word can't paw at our hearts unless we're in it, reading and memorizing regularly. We must keep it close, like Makenzie does Bentley. And we must respond when it whines and whimpers at us. If we roll over and bury our head in the pillow of denial and rebellion, our spiritual health may get worse.

Bentley warns Makenzie because she loves her. God loves us infinitely more. Will you heed His warnings and let Him keep you safe?

Hear me, my people, and I will warn you—if you would only listen to me, Israel! (Psalm 81:8)

Consider This:

Has a dog's warning ever kept you from danger? What did the dog do? How did you respond? How has God's Word saved you from spiritual low blood sugar?

The Dog That Made a Doctor Think Twice

God's Methods May Surprise Us

Our brightest blazes of gladness are commonly kindled by unexpected sparks.

Samuel Johnson

Back in 2011, Michelle's life was anything but predictable, and her surprises were not likely to be pleasant. Her husband, Tyler, was a serviceman in special ops and could be sent on a mission at a moment's notice. At least as scary, her four-year-old, Zachary, had a brain malformation and was having one or two grand mal seizures a month without warning. Still, Michelle had gotten used to living with these "swords of Damocles," so she did her best to cope and carry on. A Christmas trauma changed that thinking forever.

The family had traveled to Arkansas and was staying with one set of grandparents who lived atop a mountain. Zachary had a sudden, major grand mal seizure that lasted 13 minutes. The ambulance couldn't get to them and they had to drive down to the nearest town to meet it. On the way, Zachary was starting to not get oxygen.

Doctors discovered that Zachary's seizure meds were being

counteracted by other medication he was taking. Thankfully, they got the meds sorted out. A few days later the family headed to the other set of grandparents in Louisiana. The grandma had just seen a news story on service dogs. Michelle was realizing something had to give and applied to get a dog from 4 Paws for Ability. Her efforts culminated in June 2013 with the addition of a new four-pawed family member, a red golden retriever named Majesty.

Majesty alerts to seizures, but she does much more. She is a multi-purpose medical service dog. Zachary has multiple disabilities from his brain malformation, including epilepsy, cerebral palsy, ADHD, and a mild cognitive processing disorder. Surgery isn't an option for Zachary, but his dog has proved to be a godsend.

Zachary's left side is weaker than his right, and he has balance issues. Now he uses Majesty to lean on. If he falls, he uses her to pull himself up. He doesn't have to rely on a grown-up to help, which is much less embarrassing when he's out in public.

Majesty also does behavior disruption. Zachary's malformation is in an area of the brain that controls emotions, and some of his meds can affect emotions too. In the past, Zachary has acted out by kicking furniture or even banging his head against a wall. These days he goes to his room and calls Majesty. He has come to understand that she can make him feel better. Zachary has learned Majesty's behavior disruption commands and will give them in his own way. If he wants her to lie across his lap to calm him, he won't say "lap," he'll say "down." She knows what that means and will do what he needs. He will also ask her to give kisses. Sometimes he'll call his dog over when he's mad at his younger sister, Loralei. He'll tell Majesty all about it, and he knows she will "listen." Majesty also goes to her boy if he is crying. Actually, she'll respond to any crying child.

But Majesty's greatest contribution has been alerting to seizures, and her help birthed a wonderful, surprise possibility for her boy. Majesty was pre-alerting to Zachary's grand mal seizures up to 12 hours before they happened. The more intense the seizure, the further out her warning would be. Typically she would lick her boy. If no adult was around, she would bark until someone came. She would also refuse to leave Zachary, even on command.

These alerts gave Zachary's neurologist an idea. Maybe they could use Majesty's warnings to head off his grand mal seizures before they happened. His parents had originally been directed to give their son "rescue meds" five minutes into a seizure. Now the doctor worked out a pre-seizure time frame to administer the dose. It seemed to be doing the job; the medication put Zachary to sleep and appeared to reset his brain so the seizure didn't happen at all.

This success triggered a new idea in Michelle's mind. Zachary was also on daily anti-seizure medication. This medication increased fatigue and also had other unwanted side effects on muscle strength, mood, and behavior. With Majesty in the picture, might it be possible to wean Zachary off that medicine and just give rescue meds in response to Majesty's alerts?

Michelle looked into it and consulted three different doctors. The third one was a head of neurology. He had never done this or heard of it, but he said they could try it. Under *very* careful medical supervision, they *very slowly* started weaning Zachary off this daily medication. If seizures increased, his medication was to go back up to the next higher dose.

I interviewed Michelle for this story in early August. Zachary had been completely off his daily meds since June 2. During that two-month period, Majesty had alerted to an impending grand mal seizure three times. Rescue meds were given and *no seizure occurred.*

Let me be clear—Zachary's family did this only with the advice and consent of a top-notch specialist, and under close and careful medical supervision. There is also no guarantee it will continue to work. Nothing is static with a child—kids grow and change. But for the moment, Zachary has been able to enjoy perhaps the best quality of life he's ever had. He's been less tired. He's been able to play more. His muscle strength and cognitive skills have improved. And he's had fewer petit mal seizures, which he has every day and which, in Zachary's case, are not possible to stop or control. Michelle has observed that these seizures seem to happen more when Zachary is fatigued, so being less tired may be what is making the difference.

Majesty boosts the health of her family in one more important way. Now that she is there to help care for Zachary, her parents can pay a bit more attention to little sister Loralei. And some non-dog-related changes are helping too. Due to Zachary's issues, Tyler isn't considered deployable for special ops—at least for now. Zachary's family has also moved to Arkansas to be closer to relatives. And a dear friend of Michelle's is now serving as the children's nanny.

But the key puzzle piece in changing Zachary's and his family's health picture has been their canine heroine, Majesty. She has brought healing in some rather unexpected ways. As I pondered this, I realized God's healing ways can be quite unexpected and surprising too.

Scripture is filled with examples of this, but I would like to focus on just one. In Luke 6:27-28 Jesus says, "Love your enemies, do good to those who hate you, bless those who curse you, pray for those who mistreat you." That goes against our normal instincts in such situations. But it can bring surprising healing. One small example involves some dear friends of mine. I've written of it in a book before, but it bears repeating.

When my friends' children were quite small, they had a neighbor who felt the kids were making much too much noise. Actually, they really weren't, but relations became rather tense. That is, till Christmas came around and my friends' oldest child, a boy of six, asked if they could bake cookies and take them next door. It was not the parents' first choice, but they agreed. When the dad and his son showed up with their gift, the neighbor melted, apologized, and the relationship was healed.

An amazing dog and a wonderful doctor who dared to try something outside his norm made life better for a child and his family. God has outlined healing options in His Word that could do the same for us. They may be unexpected, surprising, even counterintuitive, but will you be open to try something new and watch for what healing God may bring?

"My thoughts are not your thoughts, neither are your ways my ways," declares the LORD. "As the heavens are higher than the earth, so are my ways higher than your ways and my thoughts than your thoughts" (Isaiah 55:8-9).

Consider This:

Have you ever been healed in a way you didn't expect, either physically or emotionally? What were you suffering from? Who and what made you better? Are you struggling with something right now that might be helped by trying a healing option in God's Word that seems counterintuitive?

Her Dog Was a Doorway
Finding Meaning Brings Healing

*The place God calls you to is the place where your
deep gladness and the world's deep hunger meet.*

FREDERICK BUECHNER

Maybe it wasn't the end of the world, but Kathy Miller could see it
from there—in her mind's eye, that is. Physically, she couldn't see at all.
She couldn't walk or talk either. She was flat on her back in the hospital, suffering from multiple sclerosis (MS). She had hit a wall, and she
wondered, "Why me?"

Then she met a goldendoodle puppy named Gus.

By then, Kathy had some vision back and was in an electric wheelchair. Her form of MS is what's called relapsing-remitting. She may
have periods of worsening symptoms (attacks or flares), but in between,
her symptoms may lessen or subside completely. She had improved
enough to interact with Gus and start falling in love, and her breeder
friend who owned him made her a deal. She'd give Kathy the pup for
free if Kathy would promise to have Gus trained as her service dog.

Kathy agreed. She took Gus for basic obedience training, but also
worked with him a lot herself. He had to pass the Public Access Test to
become a service dog, and he did—with flying colors.

Kathy has also worked with Gus on a variety of tasks. She taught him to turn lights on and off, open and close doors, and fetch, to name a few. Kathy used a laser pointer, and whatever the light hit, Gus would bring to her. She rewarded him with a treat to reinforce his learning.

This led to a humorous incident. One day Gus decided he would be the one to control the treat stream. He had fetched a pillow and been rewarded. He then proceeded to get Kathy's slippers, a throw rug, and a canvas bag filled with mail, piling all of them on top of his master, hoping they would trigger more goodies.

Gus also learned to fetch help for Kathy if she were to need it. She does ongoing drills with her now eight-year-old dog. For example, she'll lie on the floor and call out, "Gus, come. Mommy needs help." Gus will go find someone, bark, and take the person to Kathy.

But perhaps the most significant and healing thing Gus has done for Kathy isn't any of the above. Gus has brought Kathy new meaning and purpose in life. He has done this by inspiring his human to get involved in pet therapy and, with two other women and their dogs, form the American Red Cross K9 Action Team. "I was told my whole life that I wasn't living up to my potential," the Warren, Ohio, native told me. "Now I'm doing it."

Gus was tested to do pet therapy when he turned two years old, and was certified through a pet therapy organization. The K9 Action Team was an added step. Kathy was doing some volunteer work for the American Red Cross and responded to a fire call. Service dog Gus came along, and magic happened. A little boy at the scene was sobbing. "All the toys Santa brought me are gone," he said. Then he asked Kathy, "Can I please pet your dog?"

Petting service dogs is supposed to be off-limits when they are working. But Kathy knew right then that she could not come to help people on the worst day of their lives and refuse to let them pet Gus. She removed his working dog vest with a large Stop sign on it and let him go to the boy. The disaster scene settled down and Kathy realized it was thanks to Gus. Something clicked. The Red Cross needed this! When she found two other like-minded women, Carole and Joan, the three formed the first American Red Cross K9 Action Team in the United

States. It has been a magical combination of dogs and humans providing comfort to all who've needed it.

Kathy and her team work primarily with the military under ARC Services to the Armed Forces. They attend parties, picnics, and Yellow Ribbon events, as well as deployments and reunions. These events provide resources for servicemen, servicewomen, and their families relating to deployment overseas and re-entry. Resources address such issues as post-traumatic stress disorder (PTSD), traumatic brain injury (TBI), suicide, reconnecting with one's spouse, and help with money matters. Such information can be lifesaving, but only if people know about it, and attendance isn't mandatory. The dogs have proved to be a magnet that helps get people there. Attendance doubled and then doubled again when the dogs first started showing up.

Kathy has her own special part to play, getting up and sharing what support the American Red Cross offers relating to deployment. She couldn't do public speaking before Gus. MS can take a toll on memory, and she feared the embarrassment if she forgot what she was talking about. But with a service dog by her side, she feels she has more emotional support, and she figures people are looking at him instead of staring at her. She also knows if she hesitates, another human on her team will notice and pick up where Kathy left off—a true team effort!

Kathy is proud of the recognition the team has received—two Certificates of Congressional Recognition and the Quilt of Valor Award, as well as other honors. But what warms her heart most is how the team is touching lives. One place this happens is at military bases when servicemen and servicewomen are leaving on deployment or being welcomed home. Sometimes the planes will be delayed for hours. This is emotionally tough on people, especially the children, but the dogs provide a welcome diversion. People will get their photos taken with the dogs and laugh and hug their four-pawed comforters, and the whole mood changes.

Gus gives support in other ways too. Sometimes people are reluctant to talk to a doctor or share with loved ones about the problems they're having, fearing it might upset them. But they'll talk to a dog, and Gus is a good "listener." He has had extensive training in responding to crying, Kathy told me. If a person is standing, Gus may snuggle against their legs. If sitting, he may lay his head on their knee. Or he will sometimes put his paws on their knees—something he was not taught.

That same empathy extends to Kathy. If she is having a nightmare, Gus will wake her up. He'll come over and lick her hand or face and nudge her with his nose. He is with Kathy 24/7 and is like an extension of her.

Kathy's struggle with MS is ongoing, and she has her good days and bad days. Gus can't cure her of this "thorn in the flesh," but he has made her life infinitely richer, and has transformed a daunting health challenge into a doorway to new meaning and purpose.

God did the same for the apostle Paul.

We don't know for certain what Paul's thorn was, but it was distressing enough that he begged God three times to remove it. Unlike Gus, God had the power to do so. But instead, He told Paul, "My grace is sufficient for you, for my power is made perfect in weakness" (2 Corinthians 12:9).

Paul had been given great spiritual gifts and revelations, and he seemed to think the purpose of the thorn was to keep him from the spiritual disease of pride. He told the Corinthians,

> I will boast all the more gladly about my weaknesses, so that Christ's power may rest on me. That is why, for Christ's sake, I delight in weaknesses, in insults, in hardships, in persecutions, in difficulties. For when I am weak, then I am strong (2 Corinthians 12:9-10).

What a marvelous healing concept! Our very brokenness may have a healing effect. It may make us better channels for Christ's love and healing to flow through, because our own strength isn't getting in the way. And it may provide a marvelous point of identification with others who are hurting and are inspired to push on through their own challenges by seeing us do so with ours.

Kathy never dreamed the wall she was facing in that hospital bed years ago would become a healing doorway, thanks to a marvelous four-pawed friend. What walls are you hitting in your life? Why not ask God for His healing touch to turn them into doorways, as He did for Kathy and Paul?

It is God who works in you to will and to act in order to fulfill his good purpose (Philippians 2:13).

Consider This:

Has God ever brought new meaning and purpose from a challenge you thought was insurmountable? What happened? What did you learn? Has a dog added healing purpose to your life? How?

The Marvelous Blessing of a Dog's Wake-Up Call in the Nighttime

God Heals in Miraculous Ways

Miracles are a retelling in small letters of the very same story which is written across the whole world in letters too large for some of us to see.

C.S. LEWIS

I believe there are times when a dog's healing touch is nothing short of miraculous. The story of Violet and Amelie is a case in point. The healing influence they've had on each other is the stuff goose bumps are made of.

Violet is a young woman with multiple health challenges, including type 1 diabetes. She was first diagnosed as a child of nine. She also had two dogs growing up, and one of them, a Dalmatian named Nikki, seemed attuned to her blood sugar levels. As a pup, Nikki seemed to sense when Violet's blood sugar was going low. She'd wake Violet's mom and bring her to her daughter's room. But when an uncle of Violet's took the dog to train her, something happened, and Nikki did not continue this warning behavior.

Violet's childhood dogs have passed on now, and her mom has gone to live with her grandpa in another state. She longed to have another dog, hopefully a Dalmatian or Dalmatian mix. She took her time, wanting just the right pup, and one day she saw a video of Amelie on a website and was drawn to her.

Amelie was a rescue dog, a Dalmatian mix about eight months old. Her human foster mom was honest with Violet. Amelie had been sick and had tested positive for distemper. Violet didn't let that deter her. She thought, *If I were a dog it would be harder for me to find a home with my health problems.* She hoped Amelie would overcome her challenges. But if not, at least she could give the pup a loving home for whatever time Amelie had left.

Violet took Amelie home in mid-December. Two days later, dog in tow, she went to spend Christmas with her mom and grandpa. Soon after joining them, Amelie got sick. A vet diagnosed the dog with pneumonia. The clinic kept her, treated her, sent her home, and then took her back again due to rapid breathing. She came home the second time on Christmas night—and that's when the miracle happened.

Amelie was in bed with Violet. It was the wee hours of the morning. Suddenly, Amelie woke Violet up. Violet felt shaky inside—a signal that her blood sugar was dangerously low. She tested and it was in the 30s; 70 is considered the bottom of the normal range for fasting blood sugar levels.

Violet screamed for her mother, who gave her juice to bring up her blood sugar. It wasn't working. She thinks she must have blacked out. When she came to, her mom had called the paramedics. As they were checking her, it was discovered that she was paralyzed on one side. Violet suffers from migraines and had gone to bed with one. She was taken to the hospital, and doctors concluded the paralysis was from the combination of the migraine and the low blood sugar. Fortunately she recovered, but it might not have been a happy ending had her dog not awakened her when she did.

Lest you think Amelie is a "one trick" doggie, she did this again— just a week before Violet shared her story with me. This time Violet's blood sugar was 35. Her roommate helped her get her blood sugar up, and this episode did not result in a hospital visit.

I asked Violet if perhaps Amelie woke her up to be let out, and the timing was just a fortunate coincidence. Violet said no way! When Amelie awakened her at Christmas, she never acted like she needed to relieve herself. She stayed right by Violet the whole time, as if she sensed something was terribly wrong. She did the same thing during her more recent wee-hour alert. Another time, Violet and her dog were sitting in a café and Amelie started getting anxious. Sure enough, her human's blood sugar was going low then too.

Amelie has never been trained to alert to blood sugar issues. How consistently she continues to do so remains to be seen. But she has had other healing influences on her human too. Violet is on disability and can't work a steady job. She needs a lot more rest than the average person. She doesn't always hear good news from her doctors. All those things can get her down. When Amelie senses her beloved human is going through a tough time emotionally, she comes and cuddles. If Violet is in bed, Amelie will keep her company there and play gently by her side. Amelie's presence is a comfort to Violet, and her dog makes her happy. She feels lucky to have this precious pup.

I asked Violet what she believes about God. She feels there's something out there, but she's not sure what. She does believe it was "fate" for her and Amelie to be in each other's lives. But would she call it a miracle? Violet prefers the word *blessing*. "I see Amelie as a blessing, and each day with her and every time she saves me it is a blessing," Violet told me.

Doubtless a certain first-century centurion would call Jesus's healing influence on his beloved servant a blessing as well, and a miracle too (Luke 7:1-10).

This man was a Gentile and an officer in the Roman army. He was also a friend of Israel. Jewish community leaders came to plead his cause before Jesus and even said the centurion had built their synagogue. They asked Jesus on the man's behalf to go to his house and heal his valued servant, who was close to death.

Jesus was glad to oblige, but before He could reach the centurion's home, new emissaries intercepted Him. The man didn't want to trouble Jesus, and didn't feel worthy to be in the Lord's presence or have Jesus in his house. The centurion trusted that if Jesus just said the word, his servant would be well without any personal contact. Jesus exclaimed about the man's remarkable faith, and the servant was healed just as his master requested.

I was raised in a scientific, rational home where miracles weren't high on the list of explanations for unusual events. But after almost 50 years of walking with the Lord, I "see" things differently. I believe we are surrounded by far more miracles than we dream exist. And when we spot one, it opens our eyes to others.

I also feel that miracles are signposts pointing us to God. Certainly Jesus's miracles were. They were intended to relieve suffering, but even more important, to validate Jesus's claims that He was the promised Messiah. They were intended to validate His message that He would die on the cross for our sins so we could go from death to life through faith in Him.

I believe miracles are marvelous blessings meant to point us to God and wake us up to the need for His healing. Will you cry out to the One who is waiting to answer?

This salvation, which was first announced by the Lord, was confirmed to us by those who heard him. God also testified to it by signs, wonders and various miracles, and by gifts of the Holy Spirit distributed according to his will (Hebrews 2:3-4).

Consider This:

Have you ever seen someone healed in a way you considered miraculous? What happened? How did it affect you? Do you attribute the miracle to God? What is your favorite biblical miracle? How has it strengthened your faith?

The Dogs That Rearranged a Life
Helping Others Is Healing

No one is useless in this world who lightens the burdens of another.
CHARLES DICKENS

My friend Scott says post-polio syndrome (PPS) has taken him apart piece by piece, but the story doesn't end there. God has used dogs to put him back together in a whole new way. And therein lies a tail…um, tale…of God's special brand of healing goodness in our life.

Polio struck Scott at age four and put him in the hospital. He was completely paralyzed and had breathing issues. Scott got the use of his legs back first, then his left arm. His right arm was another matter. His mom worked with him for a year just to regain any motion in it, and it took three surgeries for his right hand to have any grip. Scott's spine was also affected, and he wore a corset-like back brace with a steel bar in it for years to help straighten it out.

Polio wasn't Scott's only challenge. His next three decades were, in his words, "an extreme storm." When he was five and a half, a horrified Scott saw his younger brother electrocuted. In his later teens, a parent committed suicide. There was other family turmoil too. Perhaps partly as a reaction to all that, he wound up in the drug scene for about seven years. But at age 36, he gave his heart to Jesus.

"I believe the Lord had been drawing me my entire life; I just didn't know it," Scott told me. He embraced his new relationship with God. Then, in his forties, he began having physical problems his doctors would later attribute to post-polio syndrome (PPS). This caused his body to tire more easily. His day job also became less satisfying, and by his late forties he was contemplating early retirement.

"This was a time in my life when I felt I could almost touch the Lord," he told me. He had two special prayer requests for God. One was to retire early. The other was to get a golden retriever—not just any pup, but one suitable for doing pet therapy with kids. God threw the door wide open when Scott's company unexpectedly offered their best-ever early retirement package. That freed him up to volunteer his time. A year after he retired, he got La Vie (call name L.A.), whose intelligence and confidence amazed Scott as they worked paw in hand in pet therapy for more than 10 years. Little did Scott dream that the healing influence he and L.A. offered others would also be a healing influence on him!

Part of this has to do with the physical nature of post-polio syndrome. Doctors haven't pinpointed its exact cause, but the most accepted theory involves the gradual deterioration of nerve cells called motor neurons. These cells help our brain tell our muscles what to do. When they're damaged during polio, they compensate in a manner that may make them more vulnerable to breakdown later in life. Age of onset varies with the person, as do symptoms, which can also be caused by other conditions, so medical evaluation and diagnosis are needed. Scott has suffered most from overall bodily fatigue and weakness and pain in muscles and joints. Doing nothing wasn't good for him, but doing too much at a time wasn't either. His pet therapy work proved to be a marvelous balance.

Scott and L.A. did a lot of walking when they visited kids in the hospital, but it was in small spurts. They would stop and spend time with a youngster, then walk to the next room. Scott would get L.A. to do tricks or let the young patient pet him. Since it was hard on him to stand for too long, he'd sit in a chair if there was one. He and L.A. also never worked more than two hours at a time, so his body was less taxed.

Doing pet therapy kept Scott going in other ways too. He's competitive and driven by nature. He needs to be involved in things he can be passionate about, and he gives every project his all. At an earlier point in life, he raised roses and once had 90 rosebushes in his yard. He planted all of them using a 10-ingredient soil mix he made himself. It was like baking a cake.

Garden chef Scott reached a point where he couldn't handle that kind of physical exertion. But he could throw himself into his pet therapy work. He could have the joy of hearing a mom say her daughter's chemo treatments went better when she got to visit with Scott and L.A. beforehand. He could get to see a young patient laugh when L.A. did a trick, like putting his head and paws on a chair in "prayer position." He could volunteer in the court system, where L.A.'s job was to be a relaxing and reassuring presence for children undergoing questioning about possible neglect or abuse. And by doing all this and more, his heart was fed and his joy overflowed.

L.A. is 11 now, and has just retired from pet therapy work. Scott has a one-year-old golden retriever, Eli, that he's trained from a puppy. Eli has just been registered through Pet Partners, the same nonprofit organization L.A. worked through, and is taking up the mantle. And though Scott's post-polio syndrome is gradually progressing, his pet therapy involvement is going strong. It's just taking a somewhat different turn these days.

Eli is a goofball and a lover. Scott has been taking him to a school, where last year special education students got to pet him. Eli also helps Scott educate elementary school kids about community service. And on the other end of the educational spectrum, Eli has interacted with medical college students at exam time to help them de-stress between tests.

Thanks to his therapy work with his dogs, Scott is also now an instructor and evaluator with Pet Partners. This has opened up another way to bless kids. Due to his physical challenges, he needs helpers when working with the dog and handler teams, and teens often need to do community service. He loves helping others be helpers, and they love it too.

In fact, Scott thrives on social interaction, and pet therapy has been a great source of that. He doesn't know what he would do without it. He also doesn't know what he'd do without the fun and laughter Eli brings into his life.

"People have told me over the years, 'Scott, you're too serious,'" he said. Eli has been quite therapeutic in that regard. "He gives me more laughs than I could have imagined," Scott chuckled. "He does odd things."

Eli loves to jump on Scott's bed to play, and won't get off till he's given a treat. He loves to swipe clothes off the bed and hide them. This dog is also infatuated with anything new. One day Scott was at his sister's home and a brown butterfly was flitting around. A fascinated Eli turned in circles to follow the insect, and hovered his paw about 12 inches over its wings. These and other antics have delighted his doting master.

What I love about Scott's story is how God has used dogs to turn loss in one area into healing gain in another. He did the same in Old Testament times for a young Israelite named Joseph. Joseph's father, Jacob, favored him, and his older brothers weren't pleased at all. They wound up selling Joseph into slavery and he was taken to Egypt. He lost his family, his home, and his freedom. But he clung to God, sought His guidance, and tried to faithfully serve and help his master. He remained true to God even when he was unjustly imprisoned. And even there, God gave him favor, and the ability to interpret dreams. In the end, he was elevated to the number two position in the land, under only Pharaoh himself.

Joseph not only saved Egypt from famine; he was God's means of saving his own family, including the brothers who had wronged him. And when his father died and his brothers feared he might take revenge, he told them, "Don't be afraid. Am I in the place of God? You intended to harm me, but God intended it for good to accomplish what is now being done, the saving of many lives. So then, don't be afraid. I will provide for you and your children" (Genesis 50:19-21).

Loss and "extreme storms" are part of life in a fallen world, but our story, like Scott's and Joseph's, doesn't need to end there. If you trust God and let Him use you to help and bless others, who knows what healing it may bring?

Whoever finds their life will lose it, and whoever loses their life for my sake will find it (Matthew 10:39).

Consider This:

Have you ever suffered loss and had God rearrange your life in a new and healing way? What did you lose? What did you gain? How did you see God at work in the situation? How has it been healing?

Part III

When the Sky Falls, Call a Dog

Andrea and Cuillin

Paramedic Pup
God's Healing Is Specific

Our God is at home with the rolling spheres,
And at home with broken hearts.

M. P. FERGUSON

How has your dog helped heal you? Let Me count the ways!" That's what God whispers to Andrea's heart. But when she first laid eyes on the border collie pup of her dreams, she had no idea how mightily her Great Physician would use him.

It had been a deeply emotional time. Andrea and her husband, Sam, and their three children were preparing to move back to the United States after three years in Scotland. They had gone there so Sam could pursue a doctoral degree in theology. It had been wrenching to leave their Oregon home and friends, but they had formed close ties in their new home. Now they'd be uprooting again. Andrea had a mountain of things to do, and the sheer tidal wave of emotion and stress sometimes threatened to suck her under.

This night, she'd had dinner out with some Scottish girlfriends she knew she would sorely miss. When she got home, Sam was waiting for her. "May I show you something?" he asked. He turned his laptop computer around and a gorgeous tricolored male border collie pup gazed at her from the screen.

"Where did you get that? Whose puppy is it?" she gasped.

"That's *your* puppy," Sam grinned.

Andrea was over the moon. They'd had a border collie back in the States, but he was getting along in years when they moved overseas and they felt he'd do best if they left him with Andrea's mom. They'd gotten word a few months earlier that Laska had passed away. The whole family was looking forward to getting a pup when they returned, and Andrea had fallen in love with the tricolored border collies common in Scotland. They were much harder to find in the States, though. The game plan had been to check out a litter in Oregon that would be born soon after they got back. The pups would likely be black-and-white. If they chose one, they'd have a chance to settle in before collecting their new fur child. It seemed like perfect timing.

God's timing was infinitely better!

Andrea and Sam are dear friends of mine. I'd been browsing the web for border collies. One day I came across a litter in Arizona. Two boy pups were still available, and one was a tri. His breeder had nearly kept him, but he seemed to have a lower herding drive, and she decided he'd do best as a family dog. It was his face that had beckoned from the laptop. Andrea and Sam reserved the pup and named him Cuillin after a Scottish mountain range they loved.

Andrea knew Cuillin was a gift from God, but she soon began to realize her new dog was also an instrument of His healing. She felt such grief saying farewell to her friends. The pup she was yet to meet became her focus, her comfort, and her inspiration to keep going. Cuillin represented the wonderful new life waiting for her back in Oregon. He was the ultimate carrot that kept her pushing through. She would get to meet him and love and be loved by this warm bundle of joy! And that meeting would happen weeks sooner than I had expected.

My human plan was for my friends to get settled in and then get their new dog. They decided to grab him right away. I'd forgotten that Andrea's dad and sister lived in Arizona. It turned out Cuillin was just 15 miles from them. Sam and Andrea had already planned to fly into L.A., spend a week with his relatives there, and drive up to Oregon afterward. Blythe, California, was halfway between Sam's and Andrea's families. Her dad and sister drove Cuillin to Blythe and did a handoff.

I feared the new dog would be overload, and even Sam began to question their sanity at one point. But Andrea's Great Physician knew best. God in His wisdom knew Andrea was about to be slammed by a crisis that would throw her into a sea of fear. Cuillin would be a furry life raft that helped her stay afloat amid the buffeting waves she did not see coming.

Andrea had had some concerning health symptoms while in Scotland, but no major problem had ever been identified. On the driving trip to Oregon, she started getting sick. By the time they reached their destination, she was bone tired and her joints had swelled. They arrived at night. At 8:00 a.m. the next morning, she was at urgent care. Over the days and weeks that followed many tests were run, and she was diagnosed with systemic lupus.

Lupus is an autoimmune disease. It can attack and damage any part of the body. It can flare up and then go into remission. Severity can vary from mild to having a devastating impact on a person's health, and at its worst it can be life-threatening.

Andrea was shattered by the news. She clung to God and to her family. But another marvelous source of comfort when she was desperately trying to cope was her new, precious, four-pawed fur child.

"God is so specific," Andrea told me. "He knew I needed to be home to hear this, not in a foreign country. And He knew I would need this puppy to get me through. I would pick him up and love him and he'd lick my face. I could escape for a little while with him. Sam and the kids were a comfort, too, but the comfort Cuillin gave was different."

Part of that comfort was seeing God's love for her through her dog. "God had it all in place before I got sick. He prepared it so I would see His hand in it. Looking back, I'm blown away by His care," she told me.

That care has even extended to the healing of painful childhood memories. Her first years of life in Arizona were rough. Now the place she associates with those old childhood hurts is also the place her precious puppy was born—and that makes a huge difference.

God chose a specific dog from a specific place at a specific time to help heal Andrea. Jesus acted just as specifically to heal Simon Peter. Like Andrea, Peter was facing a wrenching loss. His beloved Jesus had told him and the other disciples that He would die on a cross. He had also implied that He would rise from the dead, but Peter and the rest didn't understand this yet. Their spiritual computer screen was blurred and they couldn't see the picture of God's redemptive plan clearly.

Peter also couldn't see that he was suffering from a serious spiritual ailment. Peter's problem was self-deceit and pride. He thought no matter what happened, he would be true to Jesus, even under pressures that made his fellow disciples buckle. Jesus knew otherwise and warned Peter in Mark 14:30: "Today—yes, tonight—before the rooster crows twice you yourself will disown me three times." But along with this dire diagnosis, Jesus had offered a life raft of hope: "Simon, Simon, Satan has asked to sift all of you as wheat. But I have prayed for you, Simon, that your faith may not fail. And when you have turned back, strengthen your brothers" (Luke 22:31-32).

Simon Peter did indeed deny his Lord. And his ultimate spiritual "blood test" came back right on time. After Peter's third denial, the cock crowed, and Peter realized the truth of Jesus's words and wept bitterly.

But the story doesn't end there. After the Sabbath, when three of Jesus's closest female followers took spices to the tomb to anoint His body, that body wasn't there. Instead they encountered an angel with a specific message: "He has risen! He is not here. See the place where they laid him. But go, tell his disciples *and Peter*, 'He is going ahead of you into Galilee. There you will see him, just as he told you'" (Mark 16:6-7, italics mine).

Jesus restored Peter, asking him to confirm his love three times. Peter went on to lead the early church. But he seems to have done so with a new humility and self-awareness. What Satan meant for harm, Peter's Great Physician used for good to heal Peter of over-confidence and inappropriate self-reliance so he could be a truly good shepherd to other believers.

Andrea knows God will work all things for good in her own life too. Right now, her lupus is in remission. She and her husband are doing what Sam advocated when he first heard her diagnosis. First he wept, but then he kissed her and told her, "Today we're going to choose joy. And tomorrow when we wake up we are going to look at each other and we are going to choose joy again, and we're going to do that every day we have together."

No matter what our circumstances, we can all choose joy if we trust our Great Physician's love and His specific healing work in our lives. We can also cling to His promise of ultimate healing when we enter His presence. And He will give each of us what we need to bolster our faith in His care—just as He gave Andrea her "paramedic pup."

You know me inside and out, you know every bone in my body; You know exactly how I was made, bit by bit, how I was sculpted from nothing into something. Like an open book, you watched me grow from conception to birth; all the stages of my life were spread out before you, The days of my life all prepared before I'd even lived one day (Psalm 139:15-16 MSG).

Consider This:

How has God been specific in bringing you healing and comfort? How has this shown you His love? Which of God's promises might help you cling to Him and choose joy?

A Furry Port in a Storm
God's Refuge Is Healing

*Be thou the rainbow in the storms of life. The
evening beam that smiles the clouds away,
and tints tomorrow with prophetic ray.*

Lord Byron

Up until 2008, the name "Ike" most likely brought to mind a certain U.S. president. That all changed in September of that year when a category 4 hurricane by the same name wreaked havoc on parts of Louisiana, Texas, Mississippi, and the Florida Panhandle. The physical hurricane was bad enough, but the emotional storm that followed was horribly punishing also. Sometimes it seemed there was no relief from the flood of feelings assaulting the victims and the pounding stress of trying to make do in emergency evacuation quarters while wondering if their homes still stood. That's where the crisis response canine teams came in. They became an eye of calm in the midst of this emotional hurricane, providing much-needed moments of comfort.

Three dog and handler teams and a leader without a dog were sent to a camp that was serving as an emergency evacuation center. They were all certified and deployed through a nonprofit organization now known as NATIONAL crisis response canines. Kris and her golden retriever, Titus, were part of this group, along with her friend and colleague, Chris, and his dog, Daisy. They had flown in from Virginia to offer distraught evacuees an emotional haven in the midst of upheaval and heartbreak. Joining them from Missouri were Amy and her canine, Cabernet.

The camp was a large facility, and the Red Cross was using it to house about 500 people. They were given a heads-up that the teams were coming. Many of the evacuees had stayed through the hurricane and were evacuated afterward. A lot of people had been thrown together and they didn't have much.

So were the dogs just a drop in the bucket in that ocean of need? No, they were far more! When the teams started to wander the camp, people swarmed to them and started petting the dogs. Gale, the team leader, cautioned all her charges to stay in sight so she could help monitor them and make sure both dogs and humans got needed breaks.

For many in the camp, the dogs were a bridge to releasing feelings. A number of them had left animals behind. The majority had been bussed in and had no private means of transportation. They had nowhere to go and their feelings didn't either. They were feeling trapped and seething with frustration. People were crying and petting the dogs and talking to them. Many wanted to tell their story.

One man in particular was having a really rough time. He was feeling lost, lonely, and angry. He looked different from everyone else, and not only had lost all he had but had been separated from those he fit in with. Others shied away from him because he seemed big and scary. Doggie Titus didn't care what he looked like; he cared that this man needed him. The man embraced this canine affection and told Titus no one understood him like his new four-pawed pal did.

Chris and Daisy encountered a group of kids as they walked between buildings. The youngsters came up, petted Daisy, and chattered like kids do, giving no indication of the despair that lurked just below the surface. Suddenly one of them said, "I don't even know if there will be anything left when I go back."

There was only one phone in the camp, and there was a huge line waiting to use it to contact government services about their homes.

This caused frustration and tension in itself. The dogs were soothing people's fraying nerves and absorbing their roiling emotions by cuddling with them and climbing onto their laps.

Kris recalls one particularly poignant incident. Just for a day, the teams were deployed to a different Red Cross location. When they returned, a guard at the gate asked where they'd been and told them he'd been searching for them all afternoon. This was the day the people in the camp were supposed to get to go home, but they'd learned they couldn't return yet after all. They felt held against their will, and they'd become agitated.

Team leader Gale stayed calm, thanked the guard, and then consulted with her colleagues. It had already been a long, tiring day for dogs and humans. Did they want to go out and mingle with people? Everyone said yes.

There were extra police at the camp to help keep everyone calm, but even so, Gale laid down additional safety rules. It was already getting dark. She told the teams they had to stay in lighted areas and remain within 50 feet of each other.

Burgers and hot dogs and music had been brought in to help lift people's spirits. Kris and Titus started schmoozing and dancing with folks. The man who had taken to Titus was spring-loaded with tension and close to exploding, but once he started petting his four-pawed friend, he chilled out. Others started to smile and relax when they began interacting with the dogs. Even the Red Cross staff asked to pet the pups. They'd been away from their homes a long time, and the dogs made them feel better too.

As she reflected back on this time, Kris painted an amazing emotional picture. "I cannot even imagine what it is like to lose everything you own: your job, your community, your entire existence," she told me. "People had all these emotions battling inside them. The dogs represented some sense of normal life, of life as it had been. They could tell the dogs their fears and heartaches and confide in them. Moms had to be strong for their kids. Dads had to hold it together to lead their families. But the dogs leveled the playing field; everyone could let go and unburden themselves to the dogs because they were safe."

Describing the party that one night, Kris said, "Jesus knew breaking bread together is healing, and it was then. Sharing bread, music, and laughter lifted everyone up. Titus and I were playing the clowns, dancing like funny critters. It let people relax, let go of their fears and anger, and laugh. That one night this was not a bunch of lost people, but a family sharing pain and laughter with each other."

Kris and Chris explained to me that, in these situations, the dogs are absorbing emotions left and right. You don't just take a dog and handler and deploy them, they told me. The team has to go through screening and special training classes. Dogs need to be evaluated, because not all who do therapy work can handle the added stresses of crisis response. The human member of the team needs to learn listening skills, and how to read body language. The dogs are conduits, and their human partners have to evaluate the situation and make decisions. Does the person they're interacting with just want to pet the dog, or do they want dialogue? What are red flags that the person may need more skilled help? When does the dog need a break, or to stop for the day? It's a balancing act.

As I thought about how these crisis response teams provided a port in the storm, I was reminded of how God is our refuge in trouble. He offers healing calm and comfort no matter how badly we are being battered, physically or emotionally. In Isaiah 25:4-5 the prophet writes of God, "You have been a refuge for the poor, a refuge for the needy in their distress, a shelter from the storm and a shade from the heat. For the breath of the ruthless is like a storm driving against a wall and like the heat of the desert."

In Psalm 57:1, David records his plea to God when he was hiding from King Saul in a cave to keep from getting killed: "Have mercy on me, my God, have mercy on me, for in you I take refuge. I will take refuge in the shadow of your wings until the disaster has passed."

God doesn't always stop the pounding storms of life, but He can stop the pounding of our hearts. He can give us peace in the midst of chaos. Rather than be a "stress mess," we can take healing comfort in knowing there is no storm too big, no sea too rough for Him to handle. He knows our hearts and minds. He knows what we need at any moment. He never tires or needs a break, and if we have given our hearts to Him, He promises never to leave or forsake us.

If dogs like Titus and Daisy can have such a healing touch in the midst of disaster, just imagine what the God of all creation can do! Will you take refuge beneath His wings of love?

As for God, his way is perfect: The LORD's word is flawless; he shields all who take refuge in him (2 Samuel 22:31).

Consider This:

How has God been your "eye in the storm" in the midst of crisis? How did you experience His presence? How did He calm you? How might you help someone else take refuge in Him in the midst of turmoil?

The Paws That Moved Mountains
Comfort Is Healing

Cure sometimes, treat often, comfort always.
HIPPOCRATES

Two mountains needed moving in the aftermath of a massive mudslide. One was the physical mountain that came down on the road. The other was the mountain of stress and pain and emotion triggered by that disaster and the deaths, injuries, and destruction it caused. Moving that second mountain took a huge team effort that was aided by the healing influence of a special group of dogs.

Those dogs were crisis response dogs. Raquel and her Labrador retriever, Pickles, were the first dog and handler team on the scene. She saw a TV news story on the slide the morning after and texted a friend who was part of the crisis response. Did they want her and Pickles? Yes! ASAP!

Pickles and her human have had special training and work through an organization called HOPE Animal-Assisted Crisis Response. More than anything, crisis response dogs provide comfort when it is desperately needed. They are there to help not only victims of a disaster, but emergency workers who are under huge pressure and may be traumatized themselves by what they see and hear. "What we do is very simple, yet very powerful and effective," Raquel said. "We build a bridge of communication with people who have been through traumatic events."

When Raquel and Pickles arrived, they went straight to the Emergency Operations Center (EOC) and were given a tour. It took them at least 30 minutes to make the rounds of what was essentially one huge conference room filled with emergency responders. People would ask what the dog was there for. "To comfort you and make you smile," Raquel said. They loved it!

Pickles was such a big hit that people clamored for more teams on scene. By the time the crisis was over, 45 canine-handler teams had been deployed to multiple locations in the mudslide area.

So what did this healing comfort the dogs gave look like? Perhaps a "verbal snapshot" from Raquel will help paint the picture. One day she was standing at the doorway of the EOC when it was crammed to bursting with people and emotion. Emergency workers were taking calls from those who were trying to locate their loved ones. Raquel didn't feel it was the right time to go in, but her dog insisted otherwise. Pickles made her way through the mass of humanity and parked herself next to one particular worker. The person petted her, then answered the phone. Pickles slipped underneath the desk and laid her head on the worker's thigh. The worker got off the call and burst into tears. Somehow Pickles "knew." Her doggie diagnostics had picked up on an emotional need a human might have missed.

Raquel observed that the dogs seemed to have a sense of who to reach out to. People would say "I'm fine," but a dog knew better and would go to them. Raquel's other crisis dog, a male Labrador retriever named Bungee, who alternated duty with Pickles, had a habit of touching a person's pant leg or hand with his nose. The object of Bungee's concern would admit they really needed that. Thanks to the comfort the dog provided, they were able to gather themselves and go on to whatever task was next. One Incident Commander who was new to crisis dogs was so impressed with the difference they made that he said he hoped he'd never have to activate an EOC without them again!

Another group the dogs visited were the "flaggers" directing traffic on a temporary road built to help searchers navigate the area. The flaggers got attached to the dogs. Each of the dogs had business cards their humans would hand out, and it gave these folks something to hang on to. It meant a lot.

Another time, Raquel and Bungee were visiting folks on the east side of the slide. A woman came into the emergency center distraught. She saw Bungee, sank down, petted him, and wept. It turned out she couldn't find her kids. She'd been in a line with them and they were playing, but then they slipped out of her sight. Petting Bungee seemed to calm her just enough to explain what was troubling her, and happily, her kids were fine.

Dogs had a similar calming influence on a man in a grocery store parking lot. Raquel and Bungee and another team were hanging out there, being available for anyone who needed them. The man came up and petted the dogs and talked for several minutes, letting his feelings out—and was profoundly thankful to be able to do that!

Karen and her male smooth-coated collie, Rio, also spent a few days soothing frayed emotions in the mudslide's aftermath. One place they hung out was a fire station a couple of miles from where the slide occurred. It was teeming with volunteers, and people were able to pet the dogs and talk and debrief a little. The dogs were also there for searchers coming off the mudslide. They'd been looking for survivors, and in some cases had found body parts. I can't even imagine what they must have been feeling! The dogs' presence helped.

Two of the teams were also invited to a memorial after the slide. People who had lost loved ones attended. Once more, the dogs were there for comfort, and people came and hugged them. It was a moving ceremony and provided much-needed closure.

Comforting people in this way takes a huge toll on the dogs, Raquel noted. Handlers need to check their ego at the door and stay tuned to their pups. She always makes sure her dogs get plenty of water, rest, and exercise. She limits their hours, gives them lots of time off, and looks for ways to release their stress. Even so, on one particular day, Pickles clearly had had enough. They had been giving tours of the EOC to newly arrived dog and handler teams and were waiting for the last ones to get there. All of a sudden, Pickles stopped walking. Raquel recognized her dog was tapped out. She parked Pickles in an office and completed the tours on her own. Pickles took a week off after that, because Raquel knew that's what her dog needed.

Not all dogs or people are well suited to crisis response work. That's why special vetting and training are vital. Even so, there are limits to what the dogs can give and endure. *There are no such limits when it comes to God!*

It staggers me to think that God can comfort all people everywhere in every crisis they may face at any time. He deals with each of us as though there were only one of us, and He is always there.

A beautiful illustration of this is the passage in John 14 where Jesus is comforting His disciples before His crucifixion. He is trying to prepare them for a coming crisis they haven't quite grasped. He is offering them a way out from under the mountain of despair He knows will fall on them when He is hung on a cross to die. He is leaving them with His promise that, at a future time and place, they will be together again. In John 14:1-3 He tells them,

> Do not let your hearts be troubled. You believe in God; believe also in me. My Father's house has many rooms; if that were not so, would I have told you that I am going there to prepare a place for you? And if I go and prepare a place for you, I will come back and take you to be with me that you also may be where I am.

They will still have to go through the crisis. They will not be spared the pain. But that won't be the end of the story. Jesus will be back for them. They have His promise, and that promise will move the mountain enough so they can bear it.

But Jesus doesn't stop there. He also promises them a Person to be a bridge of communication and so much more till He returns. That Person is God's Holy Spirit. In verses 16-17, Jesus assures them, "And I will ask the Father, and he will give you another advocate to help you and be with you forever—the Spirit of truth. The world cannot accept him, because it neither sees him nor knows him. But you know him, for he lives with you and will be in you."

If we have put our faith in Jesus, the Messiah, for forgiveness of sins, we have God's promises and His Spirit dwells within us. We still have to go through the tribulations of this life, but God's comfort is always a heart's cry away. We can reach out to Him through His Word and His Spirit and in prayer. And because He knows we humans may need something warm and fuzzy too, He has made dogs.

You, LORD, hear the desire of the afflicted; you encourage them, and you listen to their cry (Psalm 10:17).

Consider This:

Has a dog ever brought you comfort in the midst of crisis? What happened? How did the dog help? How have God's Word and His Spirit done this?

Her Paw Lit a Candle
God Keeps Our Hope Alive

God puts rainbows in the clouds so that each
of us—in the dreariest and most dreaded
moments—can see a possibility of hope.
MAYA ANGELOU

It was 1996 when storm clouds first gathered on Lili's horizon. She was diagnosed with a rare and potentially devastating autoimmune disease. Ocular cicatricial pemphigoid (OCP) attacks the mucus membranes everywhere in the body, including the eyes. The membranes in Lili's eyes were so bad she had to have a damaged section snipped away.

Lili's doctors put her on heavy-duty medication, and she did all right for a while. But she became concerned about possible long-term effects of these drugs. She backed off them, and whether for that reason or some other, her health took a dive. Lili lost her sight in one eye. The mucus membranes in her throat and nose became raw. She couldn't eat. It was agony to swallow. She struggled to choke down liquid meals and her weight plummeted.

But there was a bright spot, a candle flame of light in the midst of her gathering shadows—the family dog. Lizzie was a small, adorable, black-and-white border collie. Normally she was a bundle of energy and loved to run around outside. But she seemed to sense Lili needed her and flipped from perpetual motion machine to ever-present companion and comforter.

During this period Lili spent most of her days on the sofa in her den, wrapped in a blanket. Lizzie would hang out and snuggle next to her. Lili's husband had to travel a lot, two of her kids were out of the house, and the other two were at school all day. Never fear, Lizzie was here. She would get on the couch and lay her muzzle right on Lili. She would fit herself into Lili's body. Sometimes she would sit on the floor beside her human. She was a physical, loving presence who remained at Lili's side and was choosing to do that of her own doggie free will.

Thinking back on this many years later, Lili recalls it as a dark time, and not just because her sight was failing. "Psychologically, I almost lost hope," she told me. "Everything that normally excited me was stripped away." Not only had her sight taken a hit, her eyelids were turning inward and scratching her eyes. She couldn't drive. She couldn't eat. She had no energy. Lili and her family have a strong faith, but she couldn't "feel" God with her. She could feel Lizzie, though. And she didn't have to worry that Lizzie's "person-sitting" job was a burden. Lizzie never needed to be called—she just came!

Lili knows her friends would have come too—but she is a private person. She also has the gift of hospitality. She would have felt she had to entertain them, and it was too much effort to emerge from her fog of pain and depression to interact. Hence she spent hours each day in self-imposed exile except for her dog. Lizzie relieved her loneliness and required nothing in return. She was God's gift to keep Lili's hope alive. Meanwhile Lili's doctors focused on treatment strategies and her friends and family focused on pounding heaven's gates, praying for her healing and restoration.

Thankfully, Lili did not die, as her family feared she might. She began to improve. But to this day, she must be under constant, careful medical management. She has never regained much vision in the eye that went blind in her crisis. Looking through it is like seeing through a white veil or translucent plexiglass. Though she has sight in her other eye, her tear ducts are so badly scarred that she has no tears and must use eye drops several times a day. Her eyes also can't move normally. It's as if they're being held down.

Still, Lili leads a full life and is grateful to God for getting her this far. She knows Lizzie was His provision for her. And He continues to provide loving canines to brighten her life and put arms and legs…er, paws…on His love. The latest is a hundred-pound Bernese mountain dog named Calvin.

Thinking of Lili and her dark time reminds me of a dark time in Israel's past. God's people had "backed off" their spiritual health regimen of keeping His commandments and worshiping only Him. As a result, their spiritual sight began to fail. They could not see clearly and refused to heed the prophets God sent to warn them. Finally, God allowed the Babylonians to conquer Judah. Life as they knew it was stripped away and they were sent into exile in Babylon.

But in the midst of all that darkness, God gave His people a ray of hope that He would restore them to spiritual health one day. It was a letter from the prophet Jeremiah. In it, Jeremiah urged the Israelites to put down roots in their new land, seek the good of their Gentile neighbors, and not engage in false hope. But the letter also let them know God had not forgotten them, and He would act in His perfect timing. Through Jeremiah, God told His people,

> "When seventy years are completed for Babylon, I will come to you and fulfill my good promise to bring you back to this place. For I know the plans I have for you," declares the LORD, "plans to prosper you and not to harm you, plans to give you hope and a future. Then you will call on me and come and pray to me, and I will listen to you. You will seek me and find me when you seek me with all your heart. I will be found by you," declares the LORD, "and will bring you back from captivity. I will gather you from all the nations and places where I have banished you," declares the LORD, "and will bring you back to the place from which I have carried you into exile" (Jeremiah 29:10-14).

God kept His promise. He brought a remnant back to Jerusalem to rebuild the city and the temple. But the city and temple fell once more in the first century AD. Not until 1948 did a sovereign nation of Israel exist again, and many believe this is a fulfillment of a far-future element of Jeremiah's prophecy.

There is an element of future fulfillment in the healing hope all of God's children have. In a sense we are all exiles in this life, and anything can happen at any time. But God's promises give us hope that one day we will stand in His presence, and the level of healing we will know then, and our excitement at what God has for us, will be so amazing we can't even begin to comprehend it.

The apostle Paul says we can only see now as though through a glass darkly, or in Lili's terms, as though through a white veil or translucent plexiglass. But one day her sight and ours will be clear. And until then we can hold God's promises close and draw comfort and hope from them, just as Lili once did with Lizzie.

Why, my soul, are you downcast? Why so disturbed within me? Put your hope in God, for I will yet praise him, my Savior and my God (Psalm 42:5).

Consider This:

Have you ever gone through a dark time when you felt helpless and hopeless? Who or what was a bright spot to uplift you? When you need hope and healing, which of God's promises encourage you most?

The Paw That Refreshes
God's Time-Outs Are Healing

Rest is a fine medicine. Let your stomachs rest, ye dys-
peptics; let your brain rest, you wearied and worried
men of business; let your limbs rest, ye children of toil!
THOMAS CARLYLE

It was a Family Day event at a military base. The pilot was there to give tours of his big C-130 cargo plane. But one particular golden-haired female especially caught his eye. He asked her companion what her name was. Carole replied that her golden retriever was Skylee. The pilot invited his new four-pawed friend into the cockpit and snapped a photo of her perched on one of the flight crew's seats. Carole didn't discover his purpose until six months later, when she and Skylee were attending another military event. A woman they'd never met spotted Skylee and produced the pilot's photo of the dog. It turned out she was part of that pilot's human flight crew. She'd been sent the picture as a joke, with the caption: "Your replacement."

That might seem like a small thing, but she still had that photo on her phone all those months later. Carole is not surprised. She knows small things can have deep meaning and even healing value, particularly when they involve a dog. She and her friends Joan and Kathy and their therapy dogs are a team: the American Red Cross K9 Action Team. The team works primarily with the military under ARC Services to the Armed Forces. A big part of their mission is to bring healing comfort and brief moments of respite to servicemen, servicewomen, and their families during some of the most stressful periods of their lives.

Some of those times involve overseas deployment and return and reintegration into life here afterward. The military periodically holds Yellow Ribbon events showcasing resources available to help. It's a highly charged emotional atmosphere, and the dogs have their own special healing contribution to make.

"Dogs are an incredibly calming influence," Carole told me. This is true not just for soldiers, but also for their families. Kids love them. Several may gather around the dogs at once. They hug and pet the dogs and lay on them.

But their elders also benefit from "a paw that refreshes." For example, no one can deploy without making a will. There is legal aid at these events in the form of JAG (Judge Advocate General) officers to help the soldiers make them. It can be an emotional time because it confronts them with the uncomfortable reality that they may not return. Kathy and her goldendoodle, Gus, sat in on one such session to witness wills and offer a little doggie comfort. The JAG officer involved observed that no tears were shed in his office that day—for the first time ever.

Another way the dogs provide a healing break in tension is by offering a photo op. Adults seem to love it even more than children. All one female officer wanted was a picture of her kneeling beside Skylee with her hat perched atop Skylee's head.

Homeless veterans have also been touched by the team's healing paws. The military has been holding Stand Down and Resource Fairs to help these vets. The ARC K9 Action Team was invited to be there, too, and the vets would sit and cry with the dogs. The dogs didn't care what their new friends looked like; they picked up on the emotional need and responded to the vets with an outpouring of love.

Sometimes the team dogs pick up on a need and initiate contact themselves. Joan's German shepherd, Oki, normally kept all four feet on the floor at all times. But at one Yellow Ribbon event she put her paws on a young soldier's shoulders and washed the fellow's face. The soldier loved it!

As Carole's dog, Skylee, got up in years, she normally liked to stay right by her human. But at one event, she walked to the opposite end of a table to sit in front of a woman who was standing there. The woman started petting her. It turned out her son had just returned from deployment and was deeply troubled. Skylee must have sensed this woman needed a healing paw. Her son seemed to want one too. He came to the table with the dogs again and again.

Skylee, Gus, and Oki had never read a Bible, so they couldn't know God Himself considers rest and respite essential. Our Great Physician prescribed a mandatory day of rest for His children, which we know as the Sabbath. Jesus also realized His chosen 12 apostles needed rest. In Mark 6, He deployed them two by two on an intense training mission to preach repentance, drive out demons, and heal the sick. When they returned they debriefed with Jesus and reported what had happened. Meanwhile, there was so much "people action" around Jesus that the exhausted disciples couldn't even get a meal break. Jesus, the consummate Healer, knew His men needed a time-out in their reintegration process. "Come with me by yourselves to a quiet place and get some rest," He told them in Mark 6:31.

The apostles got a brief alone time with Jesus in a boat, but the crowds beat them to their chosen place of seclusion. Still, this brief pause with their infinitely loving Lord had to have refreshed them.

What about us? Nowadays we don't have to climb into a boat on the Sea of Galilee to have time alone with the Lord. We can find a quiet place wherever we are, read His Word, and talk to Him in prayer. We can listen for the still, small voice of His Spirit, guiding and calming us and bringing respite and rest. And we can thank Him for these marvelous creatures called dogs that He created to be an extension of His love.

Truly my soul finds rest in God; my salvation comes from him (Psalm 62:1).

Consider This:

Who or what in your life provides small moments of rest and respite? Has a dog ever done this for you? How? What benefits have you noticed? Do you take time alone with the Lord to find rest in Him?

A Healing Paw in Crisis
Facing Feelings Brings Healing

When the heart is full it runs out of the eyes.
SHOLEM ALEICHEM

Oscar the border collie doesn't have his PhD, and he has not read a single textbook either. But this doggie therapist has specialized training and plenty of supervised hours. He and his human, Janet, have comforted people in the aftermath of varied crises and shown that a dog can sometimes be the best medic.

A certain older couple from a seaside area might agree. They and their grown children met Oscar in the aftermath of a devastating hurricane. They were staring at the remains of their family home, which had been demolished. Janet thought the parents looked really troubled. They spent quite a few minutes hunkered down, petting Oscar and recounting the history of the house. The family had moved there when the kids were small. They'd marked the children's growth on the walls. The fabric of their family was interwoven with this home and they'd lost slices of their history they could never replace. Tears welled up several times as they talked.

Finally they seemed to find some resolve to tackle the tasks at hand, and they walked off looking ready to dig in. Janet had a sense that they just hadn't known how to get started, and talking to and petting Oscar helped.

Their story seemed to be multiplied everywhere. The place looked like a wasteland. It took days or weeks for some residents to get back to their homes. There were no toilets or running water, and blocked roads had to be cleared. One area was opened at a time, and only during daylight hours. As people dealt with the shock of seeing their decimated homes for the first time, Janet felt like she and Oscar couldn't do enough. What they offered seemed a mere drop in the bucket compared to the need. But the folks who were petting Oscar and the other crisis response dogs deployed to the scene kept saying the dogs made a difference.

Oscar also made a difference to shell-shocked employees after a horrific workplace shooting. Twelve victims were killed and eight more were injured. Thousands of people worked at the facility and it was a terrible trauma. They reached out to HOPE Animal-Assisted Crisis Response for some special doggie TLC.

Teams were on-site in 36 hours, including Oscar and Janet. At first the teams set up in a central location. People had been evacuated from the building where the shooting took place, and the authorities collected personal items from the desks. This was the pick-up area, and employees were encountering things and people they had last seen just before the violence erupted. But in the midst of all the swirling emotion, they could also stop, pet a dog, and find a moment of comfort. As people got to know the teams, calls came for them to come and visit employees in their workspaces as well.

"The leadership did all they could to let people know it was okay to feel awful," Janet told me. Still, this was a highly professional environment. Personnel wanted to put on a brave face with each other, but they didn't need to do that with a dog. They could let their emotional guard down.

"There were some pretty brave people on the floor with the dogs," Janet went on. "They'd be staring into the dogs' eyes, talking and weeping." Other than introducing themselves and their dogs, the human halves of the teams often didn't need to talk at all, but they were trained to do "active listening" if people wanted that.

One fellow they saw repeatedly only wanted Oscar. Janet sat out of his view while he communed with her dog. Oscar would roll over to let the fellow rub his tummy. The emotion was so strong that she could almost palpably feel it.

"One thing the dogs seem to do is give people permission to be more human, to get in touch with their feelings," Janet said. "It's as if the dogs are a passport or hall pass to check in on their emotions." Another employee just about said as much. Janet and Oscar met her when some of the teams took a wrong turn. They wound up in the wrong building—or maybe it was the right one. A woman came out of a side office to briefly visit with the dogs, and then returned to her desk. Janet and Oscar wound up in the same place the next day, and the same woman sought them out. This time she visited with them longer and opened up more about her feelings and what interacting with the dogs meant to her.

Janet is passionate not only about the work she does, but about the need to protect the dogs involved. When it comes to crisis response, not just any doggie doctor will do. HOPE requires all crisis response dogs to be trained therapy dogs, but not every therapy dog can handle crisis work. "Crisis response is therapy work on steroids," she told me. "These dogs need to be more resilient."

Therapy work is usually a day job with limited hours and a warm doggie bed and familiar food bowl at the end. Crisis work—not so much. Dogs may have to travel for hours or days to reach a location. They may have to stay over in a strange place instead of going home. Crisis dogs work longer hours and deal with a lot more people, and those people's emotions can be intense. That's why crisis response dogs require extra training and evaluations. And their human partners need extra training, too, in how to stay tuned to their dogs and recognize if they're getting too tired or stressed. "Sometimes spontaneous volunteers will show up uninvited with their dogs, and they may have good intentions," Janet said. "But the situation could be way too much for them."

Janet and Oscar are skilled crisis responders, and she knows how to maximize healing and minimize risk. The Old Testament prophet Moses needed such skills too. Sometimes he got in over his head, but he was honest about his feelings and let God know when the situation was way too much for him. That's what he did in Numbers 11, when he was facing a rebellion of sorts. He was trying to lead his people through the wilderness and they were whining about having only manna to eat. They wanted meat—and Moses wanted relief! He cried out to God,

> Why are you treating me, your servant, so harshly? Have mercy on me! What did I do to deserve the burden of all these people? Did I give birth to them? Did I bring them into the world? Why did you tell me to carry them in my arms like a mother carries a nursing baby? How can I carry them to the land you swore to give their ancestors? Where am I supposed to get meat for all these people? They keep whining to me, saying, "Give us meat to eat!" I can't carry all these people by myself! The load is far too heavy! If this is how you intend to treat me, just go ahead and kill me. Do me a favor and spare me this misery! (Numbers 11:11-15 NLT)

Moses got real and faced his feelings, and God gave healing help. He had Moses choose 70 qualified men to bear some of his leadership burdens. Then God provided the people with meat—and a huge helping of divine discipline. God's intervention got Moses past his burnout and the Israelites past their crisis of rebellion. Moses weathered other crises and led his people till he was 120 years old.

Crises happen. If we want to get past them and heal fully, we need to get real. We need to face our feelings and get them out. Sometimes a dog may be the best medic to jump-start that process, but there is no Great Physician like our God, and we can always share our hearts with Him!

You, LORD, have delivered me from death, my eyes from tears, my feet from stumbling, that I may walk before the LORD in the land of the living (Psalm 116:8-9).

Consider This:

Have you ever expressed feelings to a dog or other pet that you were hesitant to share with people? Did it make you feel better? Do you share your feelings with God? How does He help you heal?

When He Wished Upon a Dog
God Sends Healing Help

*However many blessings we expect from
God, His infinite liberality will always
exceed all our wishes and our thoughts.*

JOHN CALVIN

Gilly Girl was a wonderful dog, but did she have a healing influence on her humans? It's a little hard to say. There is less debate about whether she was sent by God. Marianna certainly thinks so, and at the time, her family badly needed a special touch. She was working and trying to raise two young boys, and her older son, Michael, had recently been diagnosed with an adult form of leukemia that rarely occurs in children.

Gilly had been living with another family on a cul-de-sac a short distance from Marianna's home. She had shown up out of nowhere two years before. She was so skeletal that she could have passed for a ghost dog, except she was covered with ticks. Dog-lover Kim and her husband, Mike, took Gilly in, got her medical care, and planned to find the beautiful hound mix a home. But somehow Gilly stayed—until she chose to seek a new home with a family who needed her more than they initially realized.

Marianna wasn't home when Gilly first started coming around. She was at a hospital about an hour away. Eight-year-old Michael was getting a bone marrow transplant. His six-year-old brother, Matthew, had proved to be a perfect match, which was something of a miracle since the odds were one in four. Marianna had arranged for someone to stay with her younger child while she was away, and that's who let her know a dog had been coming around. But she had more pressing concerns, and she didn't think much about it.

As for Michael, he'd been thinking about dogs quite a bit. He'd yearned for a puppy forever. When the Make A Wish Foundation offered to grant a wish for him, he chose a puppy hands down. Marianna wasn't so sure a dog was a good idea right then. She finally relented, but then noticed how much Michael enjoyed a computer he was using at the hospital. She encouraged Michael to ask for a computer instead, and a desk and chair to go with it. She would get him a puppy herself.

God and Gilly Girl had other plans. Marianna and Michael came home to find Gilly hanging out on their doorstep. All these years later, memories differ as to how everyone figured out where Gilly came from. What they do recall is that Kim and her husband were mystified; their yard was fenced and Gilly had never done this sort of thing before. What's more, she *kept* getting out even after she was busted. To this day, Kim and Mike don't know how she did it.

Was Gilly on God's mission to fulfill Michael's wish? Michael didn't seem to think so—at least not at first. He had wanted a *puppy*, and Gilly was too old. Tell it to the dog! She just kept showing up, and one day as he stood at the top of the stairs watching Gilly parked on the front door mat, he caved to canine perseverance. "Okay, she wins. I'll take her," he told his mom.

Actually, everybody won. Kim and Mike had other dogs and recognized Gilly was needed elsewhere. Gilly captured all her new family's hearts and brightened their lives till she went to her doggie reward some six and a half years later. Michael and Matthew are all grown up now, and it will soon be 20 years that Michael is cancer-free. As for Marianna, she still lives on the same street, and still believes with all her heart that Gilly was God's gift.

Gilly made Michael's wish come true, albeit in an unexpected way. But could her deeper mission have been with Marianna? What healing influence did it have for Marianna to see a dog-shaped manifestation of God's love and care? How might it have encouraged and strengthened her, and soothed her heart in the midst of hard times? We, and she, may never fully know, but I have to think it helped.

God sent Marianna and her family a dog. He sent the biblical David a different kind of healing help. David was going through tough times too. God had chosen him as Israel's next king and the prophet Samuel had anointed him, but the current ruler, Saul, was having none of it. He sought to kill David, and the would-be king and his followers were forced to hide out and lay low for years. As 1 Samuel 25 opens, Samuel has died and been laid to rest, and David and his followers have retreated to the wilderness.

David learned that a rich man named Nabal was shearing his sheep, which meant there'd be feasting. David's men had been near Nabal's shepherds and their flocks, but had taken nothing from them, even though times were lean for them. They had actually helped protect Nabal's people and property. David sent some of his young men to greet Nabal and respectfully ask that he share some of his bounty with David's men—whatever Nabal thought right. Rather than do so, Nabal lived up to his name, which means "fool." He not only refused the request, he did so in a rude and insulting way. When David heard of it, he was furious, and he vowed to take revenge by killing Nabal and all his male family members.

Meanwhile Nabal's beautiful, wise, and godly wife, Abigail, heard what happened. One of Nabal's shepherds had gone to warn her. She hastily put together a bountiful gift for David, loaded it on donkeys, raced to intercept David and his forces, and begged him for mercy. Not just her gift, but her words as well, were a healing influence. She spoke humbly and respectfully, acknowledged David's destiny to be king, and pleaded with him not to take revenge into his own hands. She said, in part,

When GOD completes all the goodness he has promised my master and sets you up as prince over Israel, my master will not have this dead weight in his heart, the guilt of an avenging murder. And when GOD has worked things for good for my master, remember me (1 Samuel 25:30-31 MSG).

Like Marianna with Gilly Girl, David recognized God's hand in the matter. He told Abigail,

Blessed be GOD, the God of Israel. He sent you to meet me! And blessed be your good sense! Bless you for keeping me from murder and taking charge of looking out for me. A close call! As GOD lives, the God of Israel who kept me from hurting you, if you had not come as quickly as you did, stopping me in my tracks, by morning there would have been nothing left of Nabal but dead meat (1 Samuel 25:32-34 MSG).

God sent the healing help David needed. He heeded Abigail and stepped back from the edge. God proceeded to strike Nabal dead, and David asked Abigail to be his wife. She wasted no time accepting his protection.

God knows what healing we need, and who or what can help it happen. He doesn't always give us what we expect or think we want, but it is always what is best for us. Will you be like Marianna, Michael, and David, recognize the help He has sent you, and receive it, for your good?

LORD my God, I called to you for help, and you healed me (Psalm 30:2).

Consider This:

Has God ever sent you healing help in a form you didn't expect? What about it surprised you? Did you receive it? What difference did it make?

A Very Present Paw in Trouble
God Is with Us in Trauma

But Piglet is so small that he slips into a pocket, where
it is very comfortable to feel him when you are not
quite sure whether twice seven is twelve or twenty-two.

A.A. MILNE, *WINNIE-THE-POOH*

It was a huge step, but the boy was determined to take it. He wanted to go back to his school study hall. He wanted to face the place where he'd gone to do homework and wound up watching in horror as fellow students were shot at the very next table. He wouldn't have to go alone, of course. Others would go with him to give comfort and support—his principal, a counselor, and a special new friend, a crisis response dog.

The dog's handler went along too. They entered the study hall and the boy strode across the floor with purpose. He sat at a table and bent down, crying softly. The dog sat in front of him and focused on the boy. "Do you want to tell us about it?" he was asked.

He began to pet the dog. If he was petting the dog, he was able to speak. He shared his trauma. When he was done, he was urged to take some deep breaths. He and the others, including the dog, left the study hall and went outside to rest. The boy cuddled with the dog. A beautiful smile spread across his face. It seemed like a huge weight had been lifted from him. Maybe facing that room helped him realize it was just a room after all, even though something awful had happened there.

That dog and handler work through HOPE Animal-Assisted Crisis Response. They and other crisis response teams receive special training to be a helping paw and comfort in times of crisis and trauma. School shootings are one of the crises that trigger deployment of these teams. Such incidents have always made me cringe in horror, but I was also one step removed—until a different incident involved my own friends.

This shooting happened at a college. The perpetrator was taken down in the cafeteria. Three others shot on the school grounds died, including an employee of the school.

One of my friends worked at the college, but was off campus on jury duty. She returned to her office a couple of days later to find bullet holes in the walls.

Another friend and his college-age daughter had an even closer call. She was a student there and about to graduate, but needed to clear up a snafu with her financial aid. On the fateful day, she and her dad went to the appropriate office. They were missing a piece of paperwork, so the dad drove home to get it while his daughter organized some other documents. She needed to make a copy of something, but her punch card for the cafeteria copy machine was ten cents short. She wound up going elsewhere to a coin copier. She had planned to ask her dad to meet her in the cafeteria. If he had, they might have been there right when the shooter arrived.

Having friends so close to the crisis, I was immediately intrigued when I learned that HOPE teams were deployed to the college afterward. LaWana and her yellow Labrador retriever, Anise, were one such team, and it was she who reached out to the college and made them aware of this resource. They invited HOPE to send teams to a vigil they were having, and it was the first of many healing visits.

It seemed to LaWana that not just students, but also college staff were deeply affected by the incident. School personnel were suffering, and they weren't always able to talk about it. But petting the dogs seemed to bring them comfort.

As the canine-handler teams walked the campus, people would text and tweet their friends to let them know the dogs were coming their way. Staff and students loved the moments of reprieve the dogs provided. Some wanted pictures with the dogs and talked about their own dogs while petting them.

After the shooting, the cafeteria underwent repairs. The first day it was reopened, people were apprehensive to go in. LaWana and her colleagues were asked to be there and escort people in with the dogs. Petting the dogs provided a distraction that made entering the cafeteria a little easier.

LaWana explained that the HOPE teams don't do counseling; they just listen. But being with the dogs lowers people's barriers. They can be a bridge to identify people who might need emotional help. One of their last days on campus, volunteer counselors went out with the teams and distributed cards with phone numbers people could call if they needed to talk.

People process trauma differently, and some get through it more quickly than others. Crisis response teams are there to offer comfort and support. But these dogs have no power over the situations in question. How much more, then, could the presence of a loving, caring, and *all-powerful* God comfort us when we are in crisis? We need look no further than the apostle Peter to find out.

Within a relatively short space of time, Peter had two traumatic experiences with the Jewish ruling council, or Sanhedrin. The first time around, he couldn't deal with it. Jesus was being tried for blasphemy, and when Peter was asked if he was with the accused, this traumatized disciple denied he even knew his Lord—*three times*!

It was a different story after Jesus had risen from the dead and His followers were filled with the Holy Spirit. Peter now had faith that God's power and presence were with him. In Acts 3, with John by his side, he told a lame beggar to walk in Jesus's name. After the beggar was healed, Peter preached a sermon to the stunned onlookers, proclaiming Jesus to be the Messiah. Many believed.

But that wasn't the end of the matter. The religious leaders weren't pleased, to put it mildly. They arrested Peter and John and jailed them overnight. The next day they were brought before the Sanhedrin. But empowered by the Holy Spirit, Peter didn't cower in denial as he had at Jesus's trial. After all, the members of this ruling council were just humans. Something bad was being done by humans, but he, Peter, had God with him.

Strengthened by the presence of God's indwelling Holy Spirit, Peter proclaimed,

> Rulers and elders of the people! If we are being called to account today for an act of kindness shown to a man who was lame and are being asked how he was healed, then know this, you and all the people of Israel: It is by the name of Jesus Christ of Nazareth, whom you crucified but whom God raised from the dead, that this man stands before you healed…Salvation is found in no one else, for there is no other name under heaven given to mankind by which we must be saved (Acts 4:8-10,12).

When the Sanhedrin demanded that Peter and John neither speak nor teach in Jesus's name, Peter and John countered, "Which is right in God's eyes: to listen to you, or to him? You be the judges! As for us, we cannot help speaking about what we have seen and heard" (Acts 4:19-20).

So many had seen the miracle that the Sanhedrin was stuck and had to let Peter and John go.

I believe dogs and their helping paws in crisis are God's provision, but His greatest provision is Himself. Will you let Him be your help in trouble?

> *God is our refuge and strength, an ever-present help in trouble. Therefore we will not fear, though the earth give way and the mountains fall into the heart of the sea, though its waters roar and foam and the mountains quake with their surging… Nations are in uproar,*

kingdoms fall; he lifts his voice, the earth melts. The LORD Almighty is with us; the God of Jacob is our fortress (Psalm 46:1-3,6-7).

Consider This:

Has a dog ever been "a very present paw in trouble" for you? Did you see this as God's provision? How has God been your help in trouble?

Part IV

Pet More, Stress Less

Baylee

To Fret or to Pet?
Cast Your Stress on God

Stress level: extreme. It's like she was a jar
with the lid screwed on too tight, and inside
the jar were pickles, angry pickles, and they
were fermenting, and about to explode.

FIONA WOOD, *SIX IMPOSSIBLE THINGS*

B usy airports are hardly the most relaxing places on earth, and stress is not the kind of baggage you can check at the counter. But some visitors to Los Angeles International Airport (LAX) have found an unexpected and healing way to "chill." They have encountered some airport ambassadors with tails and paws dressed in bright red vests proclaiming, "PET ME!" These dogs and their humans are part of a program called PUP—Pets Unstressing Passengers.

To be part of PUP, dogs and their handlers have to get special training and work through an approved pet therapy organization. Ginny and her parti-colored goldendoodle, Baylee, are one such team. They love giving people's spirits a lift and easing tensions, and they've been able to do so in a smorgasbord of situations.

For some passengers, the cost of flying isn't just airfare; it's air fear. One dad rushed up to Ginny and Baylee on behalf of his daughter. He told them she was scared to death to fly and begged them to come over and help her calm down. They were glad to oblige.

Another gentleman they encountered was wound so tightly that he was headed to a bar for a drink to help him relax. After petting Baylee, he decided he didn't need the libation after all.

Then there was the woman who treated PUP like a cup of cold water in a parched desert, exclaiming how much LAX needed this. Traffic snarls and airport security had tied her in knots. She told Ginny how nice it was to be able to pet a dog, and got down and buried her head in Baylee's fur.

Sometimes a traveler is stressed because of a specific situation, like the dad who was on his way home from vacation with his teenage son. They'd been out of the country and the boy had started having seizures. This had never happened before. Ginny brought Baylee over to the teen, who was in a wheelchair, and he was petting Baylee and loving it.

Lou and Barbara and their pointer mix, Hazel, have also done airport meet and greet under PUP's auspices. They said airport personnel love their dog as much as passengers do. Dealing with customers all day can be wearing, and petting Hazel provides a nice break.

Hazel loves interacting with youngsters. One time a group of Girl Scouts surrounded the dog. Petting her also proved a welcome distraction for some kids whose plane was delayed eight hours—and their parents had to love it too!

Lou and Barbara have also run into people who were spooked about flying, like the young man who was traveling to meet his fiancée. His fear had an added layer: he was suffering from post-traumatic stress disorder (PTSD). As he petted Hazel he shared that this was the first time he was flying alone.

As I thought of Baylee and Hazel and how they've helped humans relax, I realized a couple of things. These dogs don't change what's creating people's stress. But taking a break from life's treadmill to pet their warm, furry bodies and bask in their love can be calming and comforting.

How much more might we be calmed and comforted by taking a break to pray and cast our stress on our unfathomably loving God?

The apostle Paul offered such an antidote to stress in his letter to the Philippians. In Philippians 4:6-7 he wrote, "Do not be anxious about anything, but in every situation, by prayer and petition, with thanksgiving, present your requests to God. And the peace of God, which transcends all understanding, will guard your hearts and your minds in Christ Jesus."

It's interesting what Paul promises and what he doesn't. He doesn't guarantee God will say yes to all we ask. But he assures us that if we stop fretting and pray and lay our cares and worries in God's lap, He will replace our churning thoughts and emotions with His incomprehensible peace.

Imperfect humans that we are, giving God our cares will likely need to be a repetitive exercise. But He will help us if we ask Him to. He might even send a gentle assist in the form of a four-pawed ambassador of love walking through an airport in a red vest.

Give all your worries and cares to God, for he cares about you (1 Peter 5:7 NLT).

Consider This:

Have you ever prayed and felt God's peace in the midst of tremendous stress? What was the situation? What difference did God's peace make? Do you know anyone who's frazzled whom you might encourage to pray and cast their cares on the Lord?

The Dog Whose Howls Brought Healing
God Feels Our Pain

Too often we underestimate the power of a touch,
a smile, a kind word, a listening ear, an honest
compliment, or the smallest act of caring, all of
which have the potential to turn a life around.

LEO BUSCAGLIA

William was about six years old when his world fell out from under him. He was a first grader in a top-notch private school. He loved it there, but for some reason he couldn't read or do math. Testing revealed he had a severe case of dyslexia, a learning disability that affects how the brain processes information.

Dyslexia is neurological in nature, and its symptoms can vary. In William's case, letters and numbers would rearrange themselves in front of his eyes. They would change order or flip backward, turning normal schoolwork into what felt like the educational equivalent of climbing Mount Everest.

Fortunately, there are techniques to help surmount such challenges, and William's parents put him in a special school to learn them. They also got him a dog. Looking back, William believes the black toy poodle he named BahBah played a huge role in helping him get through some of his hardest years.

Changing schools was a blow to William. It left him with a sense that he wasn't good enough. But a loving four-pawed pal—his dog— snuggled his way in between William and his hurt and loneliness.

The toughest part of William's day was doing homework upstairs in his room. It took hours. He kept BahBah with him, and if he felt discouraged, he cuddled with his poodle and it made him feel better.

During one of those homework sessions, BahBah did something that became a defining moment in his healing influence on William. The boy was struggling to do a math problem. In the height of frustration, he started venting—groaning and howling. BahBah came next to his boy and began howling too. William burst out laughing and ran to get his parents to show them what BahBah was doing. It seemed to William that his dog was responding to him. From then on, when he howled in frustration, BahBah howled back, and it made William feel like he could stick it out and finish the work in front of him.

Though BahBah was a "helping howl" in homework, he was, after all, a dog. In at least one instance, he got William in trouble. The boy took a break and walked out of his room, leaving his notebook unguarded on the floor. He returned to find the top part chewed off. William tried to tell his teacher the dog ate his homework, but the teacher wasn't biting.

Such antics aside, William feels it was BahBah who made things bearable in those years. Much as they loved him, his parents couldn't sit with him all evening. BahBah could—first perched on his desk, and later, when he got bigger, curled at William's feet. BahBah was his four-legged homework buddy who was always there and seemed to care about everything he did.

BahBah helped in another way too. Normally kids were only allowed to attend the special school for two years. Because William's case was severe, they bent the rules and let him stay for three. But there was a lot of changeover among the students, so it was hard for William to form long-term friendships. The one constant friend there through it all was BahBah.

William and his parents were hoping to get him back into his original private school beginning in fifth grade. But he didn't make it. He spent fifth grade in public school and went from a class of 12 to a class of 25. This was tough for a child with his learning challenges. Add to that the pressure he was putting on himself to do well enough to reapply and get into private school for sixth grade, which was the start of middle school.

During this year, BahBah the dog really stepped up his game. He sat by William and loved on him for hours. William knew BahBah saw how hard he was working, even if he wasn't always sure his parents knew (they did!).

William *did* get into the school of his choice for middle school. And though it wasn't a cakewalk, things got better. Faithful BahBah was there, as always, to lend a loving paw and emotional support. Then, in his early high school years, something seemed to click in William's mind. He rose to the top of his classes, though he still had to put in extra homework time. Now a senior, he's applying to college and playing a leading role in his school's upcoming Shakespeare play. He wants to study political science and economics and work in an arena that helps alleviate human suffering.

As for BahBah, he is 12 now and has spent the last two and a half years offering love and support to William's grandparents, who are in a different state. They live in a rural area without close neighbors. William's grandpa has heart issues and has been in and out of the hospital. BahBah's presence means Grandma is never home alone. The little poodle keeps her company, like he used to do for William. And now that he's older, BahBah likes this quieter life. William and his two energetic younger siblings love romping with a younger canine family member, a Cavalier King Charles spaniel named Bear. And William still gets to see BahBah at Christmas.

Thinking about how BahBah came alongside William in a difficult time makes me think about how God comes alongside us. Part of what we do when we pray is groan or "howl" to the Lord about our struggles or the struggles of others. And as we cry out to the Lord, His indwelling Spirit actually helps us. Romans 8:26-27 (NASB) says,

In the same way the Spirit also helps our weakness; for we do not know how to pray as we should, but the Spirit Himself intercedes for *us* with groanings too deep for words; and He who searches the hearts knows what the mind of the Spirit is, because He intercedes for the saints according to *the will of* God.

BahBah's howling was healing to William because he felt his dog understood and cared about his pain. God's Spirit does this for His children—and so much more. In this fallen world, even when we belong to the Lord, we may have times of "spiritual dyslexia" when the "letters and numbers" of God's truth rearrange themselves or flip backward. In every facet of life, we need the Spirit's healing intercession so we can view life from God's perspective, move into His will, do what He has for us, and be who He created us to be.

God's healing power is infinite, but BahBah the dog got an awful lot done just by being there and caring about his boy. As you open your heart to God's Spirit, is He leading you to be a healing touch in someone's life just by being there and caring, like BahBah did?

Praise be to the God and Father of our Lord Jesus Christ, the Father of compassion and the God of all comfort, who comforts us in all our troubles, so that we can comfort those in any trouble with the comfort we ourselves receive from God (2 Corinthians 1:3-4).

Consider This:

When have you most needed someone to be there for you and care? Who did this for you? How did it help? Do you know someone you can bless in this way?

Tranquilizer with Paws
God's Presence Is Healing

Every tomorrow has two handles. We can take hold of
it with the handle of anxiety or the handle of faith.
HENRY WARD BEECHER

When the clouds began to gather in Vanessa's world, she was only in eighth grade. It started with a period of stress. As time passed, the blanket of depression and anxiety that oppressed her grew heavier. She dropped out of school in ninth grade and completed her studies online. The next year she enrolled in a new school that had a special program for students with emotional disabilities. But despite the extra help, she still struggled so much that she missed more classes than she attended. By twelfth grade she had been to four different psychiatrists who, between them, had tried 30 different medications. Finally one seemed to help a little, but not nearly enough.

Depression had been Vanessa's predominant problem at first, but now anxiety was. It was backing her into a tunnel of fear. Normally she'd have been headed to college, but how was she going to find her way out of the tunnel so she could get there?

Fortunately a school guidance counselor got an idea. She had a friend named Kris who did therapy work with her dogs. She invited

Kris and her golden retriever, Titus, to meet with Vanessa. The four-pawed therapist laid his head on Vanessa's lap and it made her feel better. They met a few more times, and gradually a ray of hope began to flicker on Vanessa's horizon. Maybe she could handle going to college if she had a psychiatric service dog by her side.

It was a wonderful prospect, but there was a ticking clock. It was now June and college classes started in August. Kris enlisted the help of a pet therapy colleague, Chris, and they launched a high-speed search for the right dog to meet Vanessa's needs.

Time kept ticking. Chris couldn't find any good canine candidates. Then, just as it seemed he was running out of road, the search took a detour. A breeder Chris knew had an older golden retriever come back to her. The dog's family was headed out of the continental United States to care for elderly parents and couldn't take her, so she needed a new home. Emma was about to turn six, and Vanessa had wanted a younger dog, but could this be the right match anyway?

Kris will never forget the night Vanessa and Emma did a meet and greet, along with her pet therapy mentors. "Their hearts touched at first sight," Kris told me. "Vanessa was in tears, her mom was in tears, and we were also. The way the two of them just loved each other from the moment they set eyes on each other was truly a gift from God."

It seemed Emma was a ray of sunshine parting Vanessa's clouds of fear, a rainbow of promise, a gift box of new possibilities. But it was now July. Could "team Emma and Vanessa" be ready for college in time?

Yes!

Chris began training Emma, and she didn't need much work. She already knew obedience commands. Chris took Emma to public places like malls to be sure she'd be calm in a crowd. He also taught her skills that would qualify her as a psychiatric service dog under the American Disabilities Act. Emma learned to help Vanessa relax. She was taught to step between Vanessa and others to extend her human's personal space, and lie across her and cuddle with her to calm her. A bond of trust was built with every new task trained.

Chris helped Vanessa work with Emma on campus too. He talked to college personnel, explained what Emma did, and made sure Vanessa knew where to sit in class and where Emma should be. Vanessa was a bit nervous at first, but Emma not only calmed her; she became a classroom mascot and quite the four-pawed celebrity on campus.

A little more than a year later, Vanessa says Emma has changed her life. After years of missing more school than she attended, she was only out a couple of days as a college freshman. And those missed school days weren't due to anxiety. She just got sick, as everyone does now and then. That's not to say the clouds don't still gather from time to time. But unlike her prior prescriptions, Rx Emma has been very effective. "There are still days when I don't want to get out of bed," Vanessa said. "But Emma is there. And it's like she's saying, 'Come on, we're gonna do this.'"

A big part of how Emma helps is just by being there, Vanessa told me. "She makes me feel safe. If I start getting anxious, I pet her, and it calms me."

Emma often notices anxiety is brewing before her human does. "She'll make her presence known," Vanessa said. "She'll come and sit next to me and lay her head on my lap. And if I have an anxiety attack, she'll lick my face and wash my tears away."

Vanessa still takes the one medication that has been of some help, but she gives Emma 90 percent of the credit for how well she's doing. Emma is her sunshine, and not just hers alone. Other students also get a lift from Emma. They say just seeing the dog's big smile and wagging tail cheers them up. Vanessa believes her dog is great preventive medicine and feels her overall anxiety level has gone down a lot since Emma entered the picture. As for Vanessa's family, they can't believe what a drastic difference Emma has made in her life!

If the presence of a dog can make such a difference, how might the presence of the God of all creation rearrange one's emotional furniture? A group of Old Testament Jewish exiles found out firsthand.

The Jewish people had been in a tunnel of their own making. Their idolatry had brought God's judgment upon them. They had been conquered by the Babylonians and exiled from their homeland. But there was a ray of hope, a rainbow of promise. God told them He would bring back a remnant after 70 years.

God did just that. By then, the ruling power was King Cyrus of Persia. He told the Jews those who wished could return to their homeland and rebuild. Their first task was to work on God's temple, and initially they were faithful and did just that. But they got lots of flak from the surrounding peoples. Storm clouds of fear and discouragement blocked out the sun of their faith in the Lord. The exiles stopped building God's house and "dropped out of school" for 16 years. During that time they worked on their own homes and crops, but God wasn't thrilled with them, and their efforts didn't yield much fruit (Haggai 1).

It was the prophet Haggai who finally set things straight. He told the people to listen to God, not their fears. He prodded them to get back to the temple rebuilding, and they realized he was right. They did what Haggai urged, and he delivered a new message from God: "'Be strong, all you people of the land,' declares the Lord, 'and work. For I am with you,' declares the Lord Almighty" (Haggai 2:4).

Emma's presence calmed Vanessa's fears. God's presence put a hedge of protection around His people. When their enemies tried to stop their efforts once more, God stepped in. They were allowed to continue building while the local authorities sent an inquiry to the new Persian ruler, Darius. He not only blessed the temple building project, but ordered it paid for with local taxes. And he warned the surrounding peoples to leave the Jews and their temple alone—on pain of death!

Emma has been Vanessa's best medicine against fear and depression, a miracle from God. He is our Great Physician. If you give yourself to Him and obey Him, He will lift you up, just as He did those Israelites of old.

When I said, "My foot is slipping," your unfailing love, Lord, supported me. When anxiety was great within me, your consolation brought me joy (Psalm 94:18-19).

Consider This:

Was there a time when you felt overwhelmed by depression and anxiety? What caused this? What or who helped you through it? Have God's presence and His promises been a calming and reassuring influence on you? How?

A Dog of Good Cheer

God Heals Through Relationships

The trouble is not that I am single and likely to stay single, but that I am lonely and likely to stay lonely.
CHARLOTTE BRONTË

No one understands the healing value of a cheerful heart better than our Great Physician, God. His Word says in Proverbs 17:22, "A cheerful heart is good medicine, but a crushed spirit dries up the bones." Goldie knew that even before she went back to school. Several years of working on her doctorate, a stressful and often isolating process, only convinced her all the more. So imagine her delight when God gave her the emotional heart medicine of her dreams: three pounds of cuddle with four paws and a tail.

Okay, to be totally truthful, her apricot toy poodle, Yofi, is three pounds when he has all his hair. When he's been shaved, he tips the scales a bit lower. But even though he weighs less than Goldie's computer, Yofi has proved he is no lightweight when it comes to lifting her spirits and making her laugh.

One way this three-pound clown gets a chuckle is by attacking his stuffed toys. He has a fuzzy pet sock he loves to shake. He is so tiny and non-threatening, but he acts as if he's asserting his manhood over that sock, and it puts Goldie in stitches.

Yofi also cracks up his humans with his signature running style. Goldie and her hubby have a long hallway in their home. They throw a ball down that hall for Yofi to retrieve in his own inimitable way. When he runs, all four tiny feet come off the ground at once, then bounce down again, as his hind end jiggles. In truth, he bounces more than he runs, which his doting humans find endearingly funny.

Yofi's appearance is comical, too, in an adorable, heart-tugging way. With his tiny body and black button eyes, he looks more like a stuffed teddy bear than a flesh and blood dog. He not only melts Goldie's heart; he stops traffic. Everyone smiles when they see him pass by, either trotting on his tiny legs or riding like a prince in Goldie's arms or tucked inside her coat. Yofi is extremely friendly and returns the adulation. He even loves going up to total strangers.

Though laughter breaks have been Yofi's biggest healing influence on Goldie the student, his prowess as a people magnet comes in a close second. "When Yofi's with me, everyone stops me. I can't help but talk with people," she told me. In that way, Yofi has drawn her out of her "dissertation shell" and helped her stay connected with people and the outside world.

"Doing a doctorate is a lonely process," Goldie explained. "You work a lot in the archives. It's solitary. You can wind up in a 'dissertation bubble.' Loneliness is one of the main things people struggle with."

Yofi changed all that. He got Goldie out of the house for walks. When she and her husband left the city for the country the last couple of summers, those walks happened several times a day. Yofi has been her reminder that there's life outside of dissertations. He is communicative and wants attention, like getting her to pause in her writing to throw a toy for him to fetch. And he absolutely loves to cuddle. Goldie guesstimates she wrote half her dissertation with her number one doggie curled up on her lap.

Goldie recently finished her doctorate, so Yofi's healing work in that arena is done. But along the way he took on a new mission. He was such a help to her and such a joy to others that Goldie felt she had to share him. About a year and a half ago, she put him through a course to become a therapy dog, and he graduated on Valentine's Day. He was trained and certified through the Good Dog Foundation, and he has his own therapy dog vest to prove it. He has an ID tag, too, but he's so tiny it drags on the floor. So when they go visiting at a nearby hospital, Goldie wears the tag for him.

Because Yofi is so small, Goldie was advised to be careful where she takes him. He's fragile and could get hurt if accidentally handled too roughly. She mostly takes him to a hospital where he visits adult rehab patients and some children. The adult patients have often had dogs in the past and miss their pups' love and cuddles. Goldie holds Yofi and lets patients talk to him and share about their own pets.

As for the kids, Goldie knows from personal experience that Yofi blesses not just the youngsters, but their parents too. One of her own children was briefly hospitalized years ago, and a visit from a therapy dog meant even more to her than it did to her child.

Yofi's ministry continues at home too. Both Goldie and her husband have stressful jobs and unwind by petting their favorite pooch, who needless to say is delighted to be healing in this way.

If Yofi has been such a blessing, you might wonder why it took Goldie and her family this long to get a dog. It's because her husband is allergic to them. They were hoping a tiny member of a dog breed that's less likely to trigger allergies might be okay for him—but his allergy did flare. His love for Goldie and Yofi was such that, rather than lose their beloved pup, he took allergy shots. They worked, and he adores and dotes on their four-pawed pal as much as his wife does.

Yofi was an antidote to Goldie's "dissertation isolation" in a way that no one and nothing else could be. He offered Goldie the companionship she needed. Even his gift of laughter was given in this context. Goldie would not have been blessed in the same way by curling up with a humor book. Her husband knew this and went the extra mile to keep their precious dog because he knew it wasn't good for Goldie to be alone. Our Creator God knows the same is true for all of us. We need to be in a healthy relationship with Him, but also with each other. He knew it at the beginning of creation and He knows it now.

In Genesis 2:18, after the Lord God had made all the rest of creation, including man, He said, "It is not good for the man to be alone. I will make a helper suitable for him." Ultimately, He put Adam into a deep sleep, took one of his ribs, and made Eve.

In Psalm 68:6 we read, "God sets the lonely in families." Once again, God is cognizant of our need for healthy relationships and provides what will best fulfill the yearning of our hearts.

And in Hebrews 10:24-25, God urges us not to be isolated in our faith: "And let us consider how we may spur one another on toward love and good deeds, not giving up meeting together, as some are in the habit of doing, but encouraging one another—and all the more as you see the Day approaching."

Our loving God, who gave woman to man, families to the lonely, and Yofi to Goldie, cares about your loneliness too. If you're feeling isolated and alone, why not ask your Great Physician to prescribe the right emotional "heart medicine" for you?

Turn to me and be gracious to me, for I am lonely and afflicted (Psalm 25:16).

Consider This:

When was the last time you felt lonely and alone? Which pet or person lifted your spirits? Is God calling you to reach out and be emotional "heart medicine" for some lonely person you know?

Performance-Enhancing Dog?
Rest in God

Take rest; a field that has rested gives a bountiful crop.
Ovid

Here's a question for anyone who has ever stressed about a test. What low-tech relaxation aid has shown promise helping students chill out when they're "under the gun" from exams? Before you answer, let me give you some hints. It's been a hit with harried test takers in such varied settings as a college of medicine, a university, and at least one highly respected private high school. It works well in a group setting. It is not ingested, though some might take it with a grain of salt. It has been around for a while, but not intentionally used in this fashion until lately. And though active participation is a plus, passive exposure may have its benefits too.

Did the words "active participation" suggest that the answer was exercise? Good guess—but not the right one. No, the de-stressor that has calmed spinning brains and turned worried frowns to delighted smiles is interacting with a dog!

Both of my friend Scott's pet therapy dogs, L.A. and Eli, have done exam duty at the library of that aforementioned medical college. Three or four pet therapy teams (human plus canine) hung out both inside and outside the library during exam week. Dogs were available for the period from 10:00 a.m. to 1:30 p.m., when there was a break from testing.

"Students were raving about how comforting it was in the room with the dogs," Scott told me. One young man had always wanted a dog of his own, but for whatever reason, hesitated. After the first day, they couldn't keep him away. Students petted and loved on the dogs and spent time with them. L.A. and Eli each had their own special way of working their relaxation magic.

"L.A. is the professor," Scott said. He is a seasoned pet therapy pooch and has a whole repertoire of tricks, which were a big hit. The students loved them. Eli is still a pup and still learning, but "he is the goofball," Scott explained. He is also quite the love muffin, and drew students like a magnet.

Scott said the dog program at the medical college has exploded, and it's not the only school where this concept has caught on. Dogs were brought in to help students relax during finals week at a university where my friend's daughter was a senior. Kenzie told me that going into the library to see the dogs between tests was fun, and it made her feel good. And a leading private high school jumped on the doggie bandwagon and brought pups in during finals week there.

Ah, just think of the health implications! Relaxation. Mood elevation. Possible improved test results because stress gets released. And there's nothing illegal about a performance-enhancing dog, nor will you get a hangover from one. Could there ever be a better stress-reducer than this?

Yes! The One who made dogs, and us, and is the source of all life and all knowledge on any and all tests. God.

Interestingly, we can get so frazzled by worldly stress that we miss the rest and peace God has to offer. Jesus points this out in a parable He tells in Mark 4:1-20. The parable points out what happens to seed that is scattered in four different types of soil. The seed represents God's Word. In Mark 4:18-19 (MSG) we read, "The seed cast in the weeds represents the ones who hear the kingdom news but are overwhelmed with worries about all the things they have to do and all the things they want to get. The stress strangles what they heard, and nothing comes of it."

On the other hand, trusting in God and His love and provision can save us from this stress mess. Moses needed this when God called him to lead the Israelites out of Egypt. He had no idea how he was going to pass this particular test, and he was frazzled. But he took his anxiety to God in Exodus 33:12-14.

> Moses said to the Lord, "You have been telling me, 'Lead these people,' but you have not let me know whom you will send with me. You have said, 'I know you by name and you have found favor with me.' If you are pleased with me, teach me your ways so I may know you and continue to find favor with you. Remember that this nation is your people." The Lord replied, "My Presence will go with you, and I will give you rest."

Moses didn't know all the answers, but he knew the One who did. He took his anxiety to God, and God promised him rest. He will give us rest as well, and relief from stress if we cast our anxiety on Him and seek to walk with Him as Moses did. And because such faith is a process, and there are many tests along life's path, He has given us other help along the way, including those marvelous creatures called dogs!

> *Come to me, all you who are weary and burdened, and I will give you rest. Take my yoke upon you and learn from me, for I am gentle and humble in heart, and you will find rest for your souls. For my yoke is easy and my burden is light (Matthew 11:28-30).*

Consider This:

What "tests" are stressing you out right now? Have you taken them to the Lord? If so, has He relieved your stress? Has a dog ever had a calming influence on you? How?

Missy the Rock
God Is Our Strength

*The all-victorious Christ is like a great rock in a weary
land, to whose shelter we may flee in every time of
sorrow or trial, finding quiet refuge and peace in him.*
JAMES RUSSELL MILLER

For Dana, getting a dog was always supposed to be healing. Her son announced in tenth grade that his mom ought to get a pup before he left for college. He thought a four-pawed pal would help her deal with her empty nest. Little did he dream that the precious pooch they welcomed into their family would do infinitely more.

Missy came to them when she was 13 weeks old. She had been in a high-kill shelter in another state. The Humane Society scooped her up along with some other dogs, and she was fostered locally. Dana reflects that Missy was "their dog" after the first five minutes. Dana's vet thought she was a Jack Russell terrier mix, but to this day, Dana isn't quite sure exactly what "blend" their beloved girl dog is.

What Dana does know is that Missy is a 12-pound bundle of joy. "She's like a Disney animal that came to life," Dana told me. Missy is cute and sweet and adorable, and innocent too. She chases butterflies, and when they fly too high, she chases their shadows. But she is also

186

a pint-sized watchdog for her human family. Dana, her husband, and their son fell madly in love with their new four-pawed blessing, and Missy lavishly returned their affection.

Missy had been with her for a year when Dana's life fell apart unexpectedly. She went in for a routine breast screening. Her doctor told her they'd found something and needed to check it out. Rather than a needle biopsy, the doctor recommended a somewhat more invasive test. Dana agreed to the procedure. Afterward, the small wound that resulted kept bleeding, but she was reassured it was temporary. She was advised to apply pressure and told that in about three days she should be all healed.

It didn't happen. A week later, the wound was redressed. When that didn't fix the problem, a special strip was applied to the area. It was supposed to fall off on its own and the wound would be well. A month later, the strip fell off and the wound started bleeding—a lot. Dana was sent to a surgeon and ultimately an infectious disease specialist who diagnosed her with a unique, slow-moving bacterium infection. She was put on antibiotics, and when the first batch didn't work, she was given stronger and stronger medication. Nothing seemed to do the trick. Ultimately, the surgeon had to go in and clean out the wound. It could not be stitched, because it needed to heal from the inside out. Her hubby had to change the dressing twice a day and it was horribly painful. Finally all seemed well and she was cleared to join her family on a vacation. The first day of their travels, she started bleeding from a new spot near the old wound.

Ultimately Dana was sent to a second infectious disease specialist and was put on "big gun" antibiotics that could only be given for a short time. Thankfully, they worked. The bleeding finally stopped for good. But it was months more before all the side effects of her heavy-duty medications subsided and her final doctor check was done.

Dana guesstimates that the whole process went on for two years. Through it all, sweet Missy was her rock.

"Things would have been way worse without Missy," Dana emphasized. "She played a crucial role. Just holding her to my chest and kissing her head helped so much. She'd snuggle up to me and I'd hold her little paw. She made me happy. When I focused on her, other troubles receded."

Dana needed these "happiness breaks." During the year the wound kept bleeding, there were times when she felt overwhelmed with despair. Between knowing the infection could kill her if not conquered, and dealing with the side effects of her medications, she got pretty down. Missy was her comfort, and she took her dog everywhere. Missy was also a source of amusement. "She has great facial expressions," Dana said. "She does hilarious things with her mouth. She's quite a clown. And if she's happy to see you, she smiles and shows her teeth."

The day Dana came home from her wound-cleaning surgery, it was brutally hot. Her husband set her up in a room with a window air conditioner. Missy came in and lay down with her. She seemed to know Dana was in pain. Dana had to rest a lot while healing from that surgery, and Missy would hang out with her.

Dana told me that during this period, most people didn't know what she was going through. You couldn't tell from looking at her that anything was wrong. For better or worse, Dana kept working. Only her family knew what was happening. Missy gave Dana a lot of empathy and it was a great comfort.

If Dana's mom had been alive, she would have been Dana's Rock of Gibraltar during her ordeal. But Dana lost her mom suddenly to a stroke some years before. In a sense, Missy took up the mantle and was and continues to be Dana's rock and an unending source of unconditional love. Dana's husband and son do this, too, and she is incredibly grateful to them. But they can't be with her every minute. Missy is always ready to snuggle and love on Dana and comfort her, and Dana feels blessed to have this furry friend by her side.

I started thinking about what Missy really did as Dana's "rock." Certainly she provided stability for Dana during an incredibly tough time. She was also a refuge from pain and despair, and a source of peace. God our Rock offers us these healing touches too.

In Psalm 18:2 we read, "The LORD is my rock, my fortress and my deliverer; my God is my rock, in whom I take refuge, my shield and the horn of my salvation, my stronghold." God's Word says He is a source of strength, safety, and salvation in the midst of life's trials and tribulations. And He is always available to us, something we can't say of each other, even in the age of cell phones.

Ephesians 2:19-21 adds another layer to this "rock" illustration. Paul writes to the Ephesians and all believers,

> Consequently, you are no longer foreigners and strangers, but fellow citizens with God's people and also members of his household, built on the foundation of the apostles and prophets, with Christ Jesus himself as the chief cornerstone. In him the whole building is joined together and rises to become a holy temple in the Lord.

Jesus is the foundation stone or cornerstone of our redemption. We all suffered from a spiritual bacterium infection: sin. None of us were perfectly holy and none of us could stop our own bleeding, but the Bible tells us He was without sin. That is why the Lamb of God could offer Himself for us. His death was the "big-gun antibiotic" that brought us healing. He has replaced our despair with joy, and in Him the whole family of God holds together. Jesus our Rock offers joy and peace in the midst of this life's troubles and the stability of eternity basking in God's loving presence.

Will you build your life upon this Rock?

> *Therefore everyone who hears these words of mine and puts them into practice is like a wise man who built his house on the rock. The rain came down, the streams rose, and the winds blew and beat against that house; yet it did not fall, because it had its foundation on the rock (Matthew 7:24-25).*

Consider This:

When is the last time a pet or person has been your rock in rough times? How was he or she a stabilizing and healing influence? How has God been your Rock?

Calming to the Max
God Is with Us in Our Storms

May God give you…For every storm a rainbow,
for every tear a smile, for every care a promise
and a blessing in each trial. For every problem
life sends, a faithful friend to share, for every sigh
a sweet song and an answer for each prayer.

IRISH BLESSING

Life has been stormier for Will than for most, because he has moderate to severe autism. But he now has a special friend to help him through his rough times. That friend is a golden retriever named Max, and he has made a world of difference.

Max was trained and matched with Will by the nonprofit 4 Paws for Ability. Will was nine years old when he got his service dog. At the time, he was essentially nonverbal, though he had been in speech therapy since age three and a half. He only parroted what others said. He was also filled with anxiety when he was out in public. His mom, Meredith, hoped Max would reduce her son's stress and help him bridge these and other barriers. She was not disappointed.

In the two years since Max arrived, Will has taken some huge steps forward. His speech has improved dramatically. He can speak full sentences now, and his word comprehension has soared. He is also starting to ask and answer questions, something his family wasn't sure he'd ever be able to do. Will's mom attributes his progress to Max more than anything else, and told me the first sentence Will ever spoke may have been to his dog. Max's relaxing effect on his boy may be a factor, but whatever the cause, Will's loved ones are thrilled.

Max has also been a social bridge. Other kids used to be scared of Will. Now the presence of a service dog in a vest cues them that this boy has challenges. They seem much more accepting of Will and try to talk to him. He's beginning to reply.

Something else that's tough for Will is any kind of transition. Getting him out of bed in the morning used to be horrific; Will had screaming meltdowns. Now Max cuddles in bed with him, and after about 20 minutes, Will climbs out calmly. It's a huge positive.

Nor does Will find being out in public as nerve-racking as it once was. He doesn't like being in loud places or with a lot of people, but he tolerates these things better with Max by his side. In a restaurant, Max hangs out under the table and Will finds comfort in using his doggie pal for a footrest. His family was even able to take Will to Disney World for his tenth birthday. "We could never have done that without Max," his mom observed. "Will actually loved flying on a plane; the airport, not so much. He's not very patient. But Max was a good distraction."

Will's relationship with Max is starting to make him more aware of people's needs and feelings. When prompted, he will give his dog food and water. If he goes somewhere Max can't come, he'll say, "Max is so sad."

Max has been a breath of relief and an eye in the storm not just for Will, but for his whole family. Not only is there less turmoil at home, but they don't have to be so worried that the boy will wander off. Pre-Max, the county sheriff actually brought Will home one night when everyone thought he was safe in bed. He was found a quarter of a mile down a winding country road.

These days, if Will does stray, Max can track him, as he did when the family was in the process of moving to a new home. Their door chimes hadn't been installed yet, so they didn't realize Will had slipped away. Not to worry; Max took them straight to his boy, who was standing on a rock in the middle of a shallow creek, throwing pebbles into the six-inch-deep water.

Right now, Meredith is homeschooling Will, but she hopes one day he can go to public school. Max hangs out with Will when he's learning, and it helps. Will gets especially stressed by reading, and starts raising his voice. When this happens, Max nudges him. Max also calms Will by laying his soft, furry body across his boy, or letting Will play with his ears.

Max can't make the storm called autism go away, but he has been a calming, healing influence in the midst of it. Jesus told His disciples that this storm called life would have its squalls, but He would be with them to steady them and get them through. They had a beautiful real-life illustration to look back on for reassurance of this: an amazing experience with their Master in a boat.

Jesus and His disciples were crossing a lake late at night, and Jesus was sound asleep when a furious squall hit. The terrified disciples thought the boat would capsize and they'd all be drowned. They woke Jesus in a panic, but He wasn't perturbed at all. "He got up and rebuked the wind and the raging waters; the storm subsided, and all was calm" (Luke 8:24). Jesus then asked His astonished followers, "Where is your faith?" (Luke 8:25)

Jesus proved that He had power over wind and waves. Later He conquered the greatest squall of all: death. One day all who belong to Him will be free of such storms forever. And for now, we are not without help when the squalls of life hit in all their fury. We can draw close to Him in faith and let Him nudge us with His Word and His Spirit and calm and comfort us, just as Max does for Will.

*Then they cried out to the L*ORD *in their trouble, and he brought them out of their distress. He stilled the storm to a whisper; the waves of the sea were hushed. They were glad when it grew calm, and he guided them to their*

desired haven. Let them give thanks to the LORD for his unfailing love and his wonderful deeds for mankind (Psalm 107:28-31).

Consider This:

Do you have a challenge that makes your life a constant storm? Is there a person or pet who anchors and calms you? How do they do this? Have you reached out to God in your storm? If so, how has He comforted you? If not, would you like to right now?

Part V

Life Ends Better with a Dog

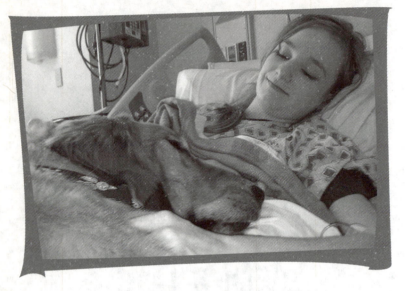

Malachi and Izzy

Malachi's Mission
How Pain Can Be Healing

The unending paradox is that we do learn through pain.
MADELEINE L'ENGLE

Pain, either physical or emotional, isn't something I tend to welcome, let alone view as having a healing influence. But my personal experience screams that it can. When I was 13, severe abdominal pain revealed my need for an immediate appendectomy. At 19, the emotional pain of an eating disorder led me to seek spiritual surgery at the hands of my Great Physician, God.

Pain is a valuable warning system, but it's more than that. It can be the path to a healing bond of empathy. Most often, this is a bond between people, but at times it may be a bond between a person and another of God's creatures. This was the case with Malachi and Izzy.

Malachi is a golden retriever therapy dog who has struggled with hip problems for most of his young life. No one did anything wrong; it just happened. At age five, he has had four surgeries, including two hip replacements, and more than his share of pain. He is receiving various treatments to keep him comfortable, but it is a balancing act and he still has pain at times. Kris, his human, would have done anything to spare her beloved dog from this pain, but paradoxically, it made him perfect for a special mission of mercy.

That mission involved a teenage girl named Izzy who had some severe health problems of her own. She suffered from type 1 diabetes and her blood sugar levels kept going out of whack. The diabetes had affected her eyes and her vision was poor. She also battled ongoing abdominal pain so severe that she hadn't been able to stay out of the hospital for more than a week at a time.

Thinking that visits from a dog might lift Izzy's spirits, nurses at the hospital where she was being treated gave Kris a call. Kris had a couple of therapy dogs, but Malachi was especially good with hospital patients, so she chose him.

"Mal and Izzy really bonded," Kris told me. "She understood Mal's pain. She would tell me when he was hurting. She would read signals like tense muscles or a look in his eyes. He would pant or rest his head on her, and she knew." Izzy had a single room and Mal would lie in bed with her or on a bench nearby. The presence of a dog that had also battled pain issues distracted Izzy from her own struggles. It gave her another living being to think about and nurture. She couldn't go to school and didn't have a lot of company, so just seeing Mal would light up her day.

Kris developed a special bond with Izzy, too—one that overstepped the usual boundaries of therapy work. Izzy would call her at odd hours to talk. The conversations wouldn't last long, but they seemed to be a comfort and to ease her loneliness.

At one point Kris lost track of Izzy for a while. Then on a visit to the hospital with Mal, he dragged Kris over to a man she'd never met. He turned out to be Izzy's father. "Malachi could smell Izzy on her dad. That was what got him so excited. He knew her scent and could smell it across the room on a man he did not know," Kris said. Izzy was back in the hospital and they went to see her. Her eyesight was worse and she couldn't really focus. But she got a huge grin on her face when Kris spoke to her, and leaned off the bed to greet Mal when he sidled over to say hello.

Mal's healing touches made Izzy's life better, but sadly, they didn't extend it. Kris got a call some months later that Izzy was gone. At the family's request, she and Mal attended the funeral. People came up and told her how Izzy always talked about Malachi and loved his visits, and they had brought her joy. When Kris contacted Izzy's parents for this story, her dad expressed thanks for "helping make Izzy as happy as possible" and added, "I will say that when Malachi recognized Izzy through me in that hospital hall, it was one of the strangest things that ever happened to me."

Mal is not the only member of this dog and handler team who has gone through pain that helps create a bond with others. Kris has a deep emotional ache from her childhood. She lost her dad at a young age, and subsequent events resulted in both physical and emotional trauma. When her mom and stepfather fought, she'd hide in the closet. Thankfully, a high school teacher helped her discover the deep, unconditional love of her heavenly Father. "When I met Jesus, I finally knew who'd been with me all along," she told me. "But it took years of praying before God took away the fear."

After a satisfying teaching career, Kris felt led to turn her longtime love for dogs into a pet therapy partnership. "I had worked with dogs for years, breeding and showing and doing obedience. But I wanted to serve," she said. She started off at a psychiatric hospital. "I knew the pain they were going through," she said. As she and her dogs eased others' paths, her own ache turned to joy. She has now been trained to work with her dogs in a whole variety of situations and feels deeply blessed and fulfilled to do so.

Our Messiah and Savior, Jesus, also used His pain to heal. In Isaiah 53:3,5 we read,

> He was despised and rejected by mankind, a man of suffering, and familiar with pain. Like one from whom people hide their faces he was despised, and we held him in low esteem…But he was pierced for our transgressions, he was crushed for our iniquities; the punishment that brought us peace was on him, and by his wounds we are healed.

Some words in the English language don't seem big enough for what they cover. *Love* is one; *pain* is another. There are so many ways we can hurt—physically, emotionally, relationally. Sometimes we see a purpose in it. At other times, ours or another's pain seems senseless, even cruel. God doesn't always give us a reason in the midst of suffering or even in this life. What He does give us is Himself; the second Person of the Trinity suffered, too, and understands and cares about our pain. He will give His children comfort and grace in the midst of it and somehow redeem it, though we may not see that now.

Kris told me recently that Malachi doesn't make hospital visits anymore. It's too much for him. "Maybe, just maybe, Mal's whole purpose was to be there for Izzy," she said. "My husband and I know that if we cannot keep his pain under control we may need to make some tough decisions sometime in the future. As long as he still wants to play and interact with us we are staying the course. We just want to do what's best for him. We wish he could tell us more."

Sometimes we wish God would tell us more too. But this much we know from His Word: pain can be a pathway to help and heal others, as it has been for Kris. The child who hid in a closet all those years ago couldn't see the pet therapy work she would one day do, or how it would touch lives, but God did. If we take up our cross and follow our Savior, He will work in and through us and give us His joy!

For the joy set before him he endured the cross, scorning its shame, and sat down at the right hand of the throne of God (Hebrews 12:2).

Consider This:

Has God ever created a bond of shared pain between you and someone else that had a healing influence on their life or yours? What was it? How did it help? How did this bring joy?

Quincy Care
God Gives Healing Joy

One joy shatters a hundred griefs.
CHINESE PROVERB

Cancer is a pretty heavyweight foe—especially if you're only seven pounds dripping wet. But a loving, loyal Yorkshire terrier named Quincy was up for the challenge. He seemed to understand that his purpose was to care for his beloved human, Judy, as her long battle with the "big C" drew to a close. He stayed close beside her and bathed her in the warmth of his love and devotion, delivering doses of joy that lifted her heart.

Quincy came to Judy as a two-year-old. The folks who had him realized their lifestyle did not allow them to spend enough time with him. Judy's daughter, Minnewa, found out he was up for adoption through a post on a Facebook page. She told me dogs like Quincy are often snapped up instantly when they're posted, and she feels God saved him for her mother. Judy had been expressing a longing for a dog, and Quincy seemed like God's gift to fulfill the desires of her heart.

Quincy joined the family four days before Judy's September 11 birthday. When they picked him up, Judy had a talk with him. "I take care of you. You take care of me," she told her new dog.

That's precisely what Quincy did, right from the start. He bonded closely with Judy and did not want to leave her. He was his new human's ray of sunshine in the darkness. When she climbed stairs, he would climb up with her, one step at a time. If Judy went to use the restroom at her elderly father's house, Quincy would circle till she came out. He did not want to be parted from her for any reason.

Such doggie devotion motivated Judy to do things she otherwise might not have tackled. For Quincy's sake, she walked, which her doctors desired. The little Yorkie also got his human to eat. Judy didn't have much appetite, but Quincy wouldn't take food unless she did, too, so she had to eat to be sure he got nourishment.

Sweet Quincy even had a way of making sure his human got her rest. At times Judy would stay up and worry and fret. Quincy was having none of it. He'd sit on her and snuggle up as if to say, "Time to go to bed." When she gave in and climbed under the covers, he'd sleep on top of her back, spooning, cuddling right against her.

Quincy also seemed to know when Judy needed other humans' help. Minnewa was her mom's caregiver and shared a room with her, but she put up a partition to provide some privacy. Judy wouldn't always want to bother her daughter if she was feeling ill. Never fear, Quincy was there, and he was tuned in to Judy's needs. He'd come out from behind the partition and give Minnewa a certain look. He never barked, but that look cued Minnewa to check on her mom. He also seemed to know when Judy was hurting, and would go to her and lick her or put his head under her hand. The welcome distraction of petting Quincy and being loved by him helped Judy deal with her pain.

Quincy's presence made it possible for Minnewa to get some much-needed breaks. For instance, her mom had long been doing once-a-week art therapy. Quincy started going along, and Minnewa felt she could leave for short periods as long as Quincy was by Judy's side. Quincy also kept Judy from sliding into the depths of depression; she had to keep going for her four-pawed pal.

It was Judy's hope to get better and certify Quincy as a therapy dog so they could share his caring gifts with others. It was not to be. Judy's health slid and she was hospitalized three different times. Quincy was able to visit her because he was classified as a service dog. Even with that classification, he was not supposed to be in ICU. On one particular occasion, when it seemed the end had arrived, Judy woke up after two days. Her first words were, "Where's my dog?"

Judy stepped into the presence of God in August 2015—but not before making it quite clear where Quincy should be. She knew that, of all her family members, Minnewa would have the most time for him, and Minnewa was delighted to oblige. Quincy grieved right along with other family, and at the memorial service he took his place in the receiving line, tucked under Minnewa's arm. He continues to provide love and comfort, and Minnewa feels that having Quincy is like having a piece of her mom.

As I think of Quincy's healing touch, the word that comes to mind is *joy*. Quincy brought joy in the midst of pain and loss. God wants to give His children healing joy in the midst of life's trials and tribulations. In James 1:2-4 we read, "Consider it pure joy, my brothers and sisters, whenever you face trials of many kinds, because you know that the testing of your faith produces perseverance. Let perseverance finish its work so that you may be mature and complete, not lacking anything."

Judy persevered for 17 years in her battle against cancer. She did it so she could be there for her family. She ran the race God set before her and, at the end, God used a tiny dog to give doses of joy as she crossed the finish line into His arms.

Whatever your race, God knows your pain and is waiting to give you doses of joy to ease you across the finish line to Him. Will you receive His joy so you can finish well, like Judy did?

The joy of the LORD *is your strength (Nehemiah 8:10).*

Consider This:

Has a pet or person ever brought you doses of joy in the midst of pain and loss? How did they do this? How did it lift your heart? How has the joy of the Lord been your strength?

Healing Angel in Fur
God's Caring Is Healing

Angels descending bring from above
Echoes of mercy, whispers of love.
Fanny J. Crosby, "Blessed Assurance"

If you'd asked Andre if he was an angel, he wouldn't have said yes in so many words. Chances are, he'd have made eye contact or jumped onto your lap instead. And he very well might have given you a paw or a lick. Those were his signature ways of connecting, and he was quite intentional about it. Then, when he'd finished brightening your day, he'd have padded off to find the next object of his doggie affection. Because, you see, angels are quite busy, even the ones who wear fur.

Jack and Pamela were Andre's humans. Well, okay, they weren't his *first* humans, but they were the ones who dubbed him an angel in a poodle suit. Pamela wrote a book titled *Angel in a Poodle Suit,* and it made Andre famous. He didn't care too much about that, but what did make his curly fur tingle was getting to meet schoolchildren all over Arizona. That's because he was chosen to be part of a program called Character Counts, and his story helped inspire kids to care about others, like he did. Once he showed them how wonderful it was to reach out and lift others' spirits, they couldn't help but want to do that too.

They'd be asked, "What did you learn from Andre's story? What will you do today to be more like him?" And they'd say, "Be nice to my little brother" or, "Share my toys."

Jack and Pamela first met Andre at a party at a friend's house. The little toy poodle plopped into Jack's arms. It was love at first doggie kiss. Andre was the friend's daughter's dog, but she was heading off to college and her parents were feeling as though Andre needed a new home. Jack knew he and Pamela needed this dog, and the match was made.

It was Pamela's idea to write the book, and a friend got her into book fairs and schools. Andre had a way of finding those who needed him most. In one school he made the rounds and ended up on the lap of a child who often seemed lost and stuck. The principal was astonished that out of 300 kids, Andre had found that one!

Andre was equally perceptive with adults. He was with his humans at a dinner party where one of the other guests had had a prior bad experience with a dog. Andre was moving from lap to lap and the poor woman started to spook. Andre licked the woman's spoon, reached out his paw to her, and ultimately jumped onto her lap too. Her attitude did a total about-face, and she wanted to take him home with her.

Andre was a doggie old man of 15 when he had a stroke and had to be put down. It seemed his healing work in this world was done. It wasn't. Little did his humans guess that he would reach a paw back from the grave to ease Pamela's passing from ovarian cancer at age 45.

By then Pamela and Jack lived in Utah. They'd gone to the 2002 Olympics and fallen in love with a certain house on a hill. They had moved there, and doctors found the cancer shortly afterward.

Looking back, Jack feels that losing Andre helped prepare them for Pamela's passing, but Andre's role went deeper. Although Andre no longer walked this earth, he was very much alive in Pamela's heart. At some point, Jack realized their beloved angel in a poodle suit might help her through this difficult journey. Andre had been laid to rest in their backyard. Jack asked Pamela if she'd like Andre to be buried in the coffin with her. "Can we do that?" she gasped.

Pamela passed on a day that began with dark clouds in the sky. At a certain point they parted and the sun shone through. Pamela moved through the doors of heaven, and a small wooden box in her coffin fulfilled her dying wish.

I have to think Andre would have loved that! He was all about blessing people and meeting their needs. He was all about giving love and comfort. And one last time, he was able to do that for his beloved Pamela. In a most unexpected and unique way, Andre was able to sustain her through an incredibly rough time in her life, which surely fits the job description of an angelic messenger from God.

God sent an angelic messenger to help Jack too. It was not one he really wanted at first. But he eventually opened up to God's blessing, and he is now married to a wonderful woman named Julie.

I believe Andre was not only an angel in a poodle suit, but a healing gift from God pointing to a deeper truth. God cares about each and every one of us, knows how we're hurting, and seeks us out to meet our deepest needs.

Jesus, God in human form, surely did this, even when He knew it would stir up trouble—as it did when He healed a crippled woman in a synagogue on the Sabbath.

> Jesus was teaching...and a woman was there who had been crippled by a spirit for eighteen years. She was bent over and could not straighten up at all. When Jesus saw her, he called her forward and said to her, "Woman, you are set free from your infirmity." Then he put his hands on her, and immediately she straightened up and praised God (Luke 13:10-13).

Most of the onlookers were thrilled, but the synagogue's leader was incensed that Jesus did "work" on the Sabbath. Um...make that *God's work*! Jesus pointed out that people met their animals' needs on the Sabbath, so why shouldn't He help a hurting human then?

Jesus was caring and intentional not just with this woman, but with a multitude of others. His love and compassion drove Him to help them. Matthew 9:35-36 (MSG) puts it this way:

Then Jesus made a circuit of all the towns and villages. He taught in their meeting places, reported kingdom news, and healed their diseased bodies, healed their bruised and hurt lives. When he looked out over the crowds, his heart broke. So confused and aimless they were, like sheep with no shepherd.

But Jesus's deepest healing effort was yet to come. Jesus conquered death, left His grave clothes behind, and ascended to the Father. As much as Pamela's passing was eased by the promise of Andre being buried with her, her greatest comfort—and that of all who have given their hearts to Christ—was the promise of being raised to spend eternity with God.

Meanwhile He longs for us to be intentional to reach out to others with a healing touch, not in our strength, but in His. Wouldn't you like to be more like Jesus and Andre?

We all, who with unveiled faces contemplate the Lord's glory, are being transformed into his image with ever-increasing glory, which comes from the Lord, who is the Spirit (2 Corinthians 3:18).

Consider This:

How have you been touched and healed by people who were like Andre and Jesus? How could you be a healing influence by being more like them?

Dogs That Brightened Fading Lives

God Heals to the End

May you live all the days of your life.
JONATHAN SWIFT

Cynthia's work as a visiting nurse didn't take her to patients in the bloom of health. Most often, they were older and their health and lives were fading. But for a couple of her charges, the presence of a beloved dog perked them up in one way or another. For a brief time or a not-so-brief time, the healing touch of a dog's loving paw slowed the curtain falling on their lives and brought some sunshine in. And what a difference it made!

One patient Cynthia saw for a while had recently lost his wife. His illness worsened after her passing. But shortly after her death, he got a small dog, and that pup became something of a four-pawed caregiver. The dog was always with him. It sat on his lap and sometimes snuggled with him in bed. The pup provided him with a reason to live.

The effects were both physical and mental. The man was motivated to work harder on his physical health. He was better about his diet, medications, and physical therapy. Mentally, he told Cynthia, his canine companion made him feel so much more at peace.

Another patient perked up by a dog was a woman with Alzheimer's. She did not remember anyone in her family, but she did recognize the family pooch. She would sit in a chair, call the dog to her, and rub her furry friend all over. While they interacted, she seemed almost normal. Afterward, her memory would be gone again.

One thing these two examples teach is that, even in the twilight of life, one can love and be loved by a dog, and it can be healing. The same is true of loving and being loved by God. Perhaps there is no more poignant example than the story of the thief on the cross. We don't know if he was old, but we do know his time was up.

Actually, there were two thieves, one hanging on either side of Jesus, when He was being crucified. One was rude and disrespectful. He sneered, "Aren't you the Messiah? Save yourself and us!" (Luke 23:39).

Not so the other thief. In the midst of blinding pain, dangling over the abyss of eternal separation from God, he allowed the healing touch of Christ's sacrificial love to slow his falling curtain. He confessed his own sin and Jesus's innocence. And then he pleaded, "Jesus, remember me when you come into your kingdom" (Luke 23:42).

Jesus's response? "Truly I tell you, today you will be with me in paradise" (Luke 23:43).

Cynthia's patients had their falling curtains slowed in one way or another by loving dogs. Jesus did infinitely more. For that thief and all who receive Him, He has shattered the curtain of death and transformed our passage out of this world into a pathway to eternal life, where blessings too wonderful to even begin to imagine await all God's children.

Which thief will you join?

Repent, then, and turn to God, so that your sins may be wiped out, that times of refreshing may come from the Lord (Acts 3:19).

Consider This:

Have you or someone you know had a health slide slowed or reversed by the love of a dog? What was the health problem? How did the dog make a difference? Are there people you need to tell about Jesus before their curtain falls?

Ridge the Bridge
A Healing Bridge in Loss

*I did not know how to reach him, how to catch up
with him... The land of tears is so mysterious.*
ANTOINE DE SAINT-EXUPÉRY, *THE LITTLE PRINCE*

Donna felt Ridge needed her. She didn't realize that one day she would need him even more. It's a blessing that we don't always know the future . . . and God does.

Ridge is a dog. A Weimaraner to be exact. Donna first learned about him through an ad in *PennySaver*. What's interesting about that is, she hadn't looked at one of those in years. The ad explained that Ridge's humans, Barbara and Denny, needed to re-home him. Donna had two dogs, three fenced acres, and plenty of room. She also had an inner sense that she should reach out.

Donna called Barbara, and they had a lovely conversation. Donna learned that one of Barbara's sons had rescued Ridge. But the family's circumstances had changed, and Ridge wasn't getting enough human attention. He was barking his displeasure at being home alone too much. Barbara was hoping to place him with people who could give him more company. Donna's situation sounded promising, and she offered to bring Ridge over for a meet and greet.

Ridge relieved himself on Donna's couch. She figured that was his way of saying, "This is my territory now." He also just about wagged his tail off. He had a great time playing with Donna's four-month-old Weimaraner puppy, and her 12-year-old Doberman loved him too. Donna realized she had herself a new dog.

As it turned out, she and her husband, Vic, also had themselves some new best friends. The two couples both loved God, and they grew to love each other. They were soon sharing church, dinners, and charity involvements. About four years passed. Life was good. And then, in a moment, life changed forever.

Lightning struck in Donna's kitchen. Vic suffered a brain hemorrhage and died. He was an otherwise fit and healthy 72 years old. He and Donna had been married for 34 years. Now, suddenly, he was gone.

It was a big transition. Donna had a grown son, but his job took him away for three months at a time. Suddenly she was the one home alone, except for her pets, which now included four dogs, three horses, and one very verbal parrot.

Thankfully, the dogs were there for her. They seemed to know Vic wasn't coming back, and they stepped in. Before Vic's death, they had slept on a twin bed at the foot of their humans' king bed. Now Ridge slept on Vic's pillow with his head touching Donna's head. She learned to sleep that way too. The other dogs moved up to the king bed also, and together they watched over her at night.

All the dogs are attentive to Donna, but Ridge is particularly so. "He looks straight at me. He's such a lover," she told me. "He's a comforter. He pushes against me. He comes and lays his head across my neck or chest," she said.

"If I hadn't had these dogs, especially Ridge, I don't know what would have happened," Donna added. "There's no question I healed more quickly because of them. They've made things so much easier on me." She also feels much safer with the dogs there, and they've let her know they are there to protect her. Among other things, they give every visitor the "sniff test." She'd never thought about safety that much with Vic around, but it's different now. Thanks to the dogs, she has peace of mind. And when she leaves, she tells them where she's going, how long she'll be, and when she'll return. At the least, it makes her feel good to do that.

Barbara and Denny have also been a wonderful support to her in all of this. "They're such a blessing in my life, and that blessing came through Ridge," she reflected.

Ridge and her other dogs have been a bridge over Donna's troubled waters to the new life God has for her now. She knows God gave him to her, and she's grateful. The Israelites of old also needed a healing bridge over loss, and God gave it to them in the person of a leader named Joshua.

Like Ridge, Joshua had been on the scene for a while before he was called to step up. He'd been Moses's aide since he was a young man. He was one of 12 spies Moses sent into Canaan, and only he and Caleb urged the people to trust God and move forward. When they balked and a whole generation died wandering in the wilderness, he and Caleb were spared. But as central a role as he played, Joshua was not the main man God's chosen people depended on. Their "Vic" was Moses—and they were about to lose him.

Unlike Vic's, Moses's death was no shock. For one thing, he was 120 years old. For another, because of a prior act of disobedience, God had told him he wouldn't get to enter the Promised Land. He was allowed to go up on a mountain and look out over it, and then he died and God buried him—just where, no one knows (Deuteronomy 34).

The Israelites went into mourning for 30 days. But God had provided a handpicked successor. Joshua moved up from the "twin bed" to the "king bed" of leadership. He was first in command under God. He provided a much-needed spiritual healing touch by "getting on Moses's pillow" and echoing the great prophet's warnings to keep all God's commands and steer clear of idolatry. Joshua also took responsibility for keeping the people safe—if they would only do what he said, and what God said. Under Joshua, the Israelites did indeed conquer Canaan, but they didn't stay faithful to God, and they suffered for it.

When I think of Joshua and Ridge, I think of God's mercy and care for us. He longs for us to love Him most, and first. But He understands that we humans may need more tangible healing bridges over loss, and He prepares and provides just the right ones. I experienced this firsthand when my mom died. I'd lost my father decades earlier, and I am an only child. I always thought that when I lost Mom, I'd feel like an orphan. But it turned out that some close friends God had placed in my life many years before needed sanctuary in a time of transition. Three months after Mom passed away, they moved in with me. They stayed for just over a year—the very year I was winding up Mom's affairs.

Are you facing grief and loss? God knew it was coming, even if you didn't. And the same God who cared for the Israelites, and Donna and me, cares for you. Trust in Him and He will provide the bridge you need to cross your troubled waters and walk toward your future, hand in hand with Him!

When we came into Macedonia, we had no rest, but we were harassed at every turn—conflicts on the outside, fears within. But God, who comforts the downcast, comforted us by the coming of Titus, and not only by his coming but also by the comfort you had given him. He told us about your longing for me, your deep sorrow, your ardent concern for me, so that my joy was greater than ever (2 Corinthians 7:5-7).

Consider This:

Has God ever provided a pet or person who was a bridge for you over troubled waters of grief and loss? How did that pet or person comfort you? What did you learn about yourself, and God? Is God calling you to be a bridge for someone else?

Watchdog of Health
God's Watchmen Bring Healing

In warning there is strength.
LEW WALLACE, *BEN-HUR*

Some of the best health insurance my mom had in her final years was her devoted Pekepoo dog, Pixie. He was part Pekingese, part poodle, and all love. Their hearts were twined, he was tuned to her needs, and when she needed help, he flew to her aid and functioned as a living, breathing nurse's call button.

My friend Hana was one of Mom's nurses, and she recalls how this worked. Mom's bedroom was at the back of her house. The kitchen was some distance away at the end of a long hall. If Mom and Hana were alone and Mom got hungry, she would send Hana to fix her a snack while Pixie stayed behind. Hana was never gone long, but now and then, something went amiss with Mom, and Pixie was off like a shot to fetch her caregiver.

The first time an agitated Pixie ran to Hana in the kitchen, Hana wasn't sure what was going on. Then Mom called the kitchen phone from her bedroom. Hana realized Pixie had been trying to tell her Mom needed her, and she paid close attention from then on.

Once Pixie fetched her when Mom had fallen. Hana found her

on the floor. Fortunately, though she was sore for a few days, no lasting damage was done. In other instances, the need Pixie sensed was more emotional. Mom was up in years, in failing health, and dealing with her own mortality. Fear could slam her at odd moments, and she needed someone with her right then. Pixie was so sensitive to her that he picked up on her anxiety and did his doggie best to get her help. There were also those moments when Mom just started not feeling well. Whatever it was, Hana knew if Pixie came running to the kitchen acting anxious and distressed, she needed to go check on Mom right away.

It was quite clear when Pixie was worried, because he acted very differently when all was well with Mom. He would lie calmly on the floor next to her. He was a rather effective barometer of how she was doing, and she adored him for it.

Knowing Pixie would get help if needed had to be a comfort to Mom, and it was reassuring for Hana too. She felt better being sent to the kitchen knowing Pixie would come and let her know if Mom was in trouble. I believe a bond was forged between Hana and Pixie during that time, one that took an unexpected turn when Mom passed away.

There was a transition period after Mom's death. I invited Hana to remain at Mom's house for a few months, and she was happy to accept. I was also trying to figure out the best home for Pixie (I already had a full house, pet-wise), and while that was in process, it seemed best for him to remain where he had spent almost his whole life.

I had a caretaker couple on the property, too, so Hana and Pixie weren't there alone. But one weekend the caretakers went out of town. Hana felt a little nervous being by herself. She saw that Pixie looked a little lost too. She took him to her bedroom and put a dog bed on the floor for him. He was happy there. From then on, he stayed with her at night. She never felt afraid after that; she figured if anyone came around he'd bark and let her know. In that way, Pixie brought her peace of mind, which was healing too.

I wound up re-homing Pixie with a cousin, but it didn't work out.

Ultimately Pixie went to live with Hana, who by then had relocated. He filled a void in her life she didn't even realize she had, and was happy to spend his later years with her and her family.

As I pondered Pixie calling Hana back to Mom, it seemed that he functioned as a sort of "watchdog of health." Israel's prophets did, too, but somewhat differently. God specifically charged them with calling the Israelites back to Him, but it was for *their* health benefit, not His. In Ezekiel 33:7,11 (MSG), God told the prophet,

> You, son of man, are the watchman. I've made you a watchman for Israel. The minute you hear a message from me, warn them…Tell them, "As sure as I am the living God, I take no pleasure from the death of the wicked. I want the wicked to change their ways and live. Turn your life around! Reverse your evil ways! Why die, Israel?"

That call to healing and spiritual health wasn't just for the Israelites of old. It's for all peoples of every generation. God is beckoning all of us, even those who have strayed infinitely farther than down the hall to the kitchen. I believe Mom heeded God's call by putting her faith in Yeshua (Jesus), her Messiah. I believe she was resting in God's arms as her life was ending and He comforted her in ways no human could. Hana and I were both at her side when she passed peacefully from this world, and we look forward to seeing her again at God's throne.

The watchmen shout and sing with joy, for before their very eyes they see the Lord *returning to Jerusalem. Let the ruins of Jerusalem break into joyful song, for the* Lord *has comforted his people. He has redeemed Jerusalem (Isaiah 52:8-9 NLT).*

Consider This:

Have you wandered "down the hall to the kitchen" in your spiritual life? How has this affected your spiritual health? What watchmen has He sent to call you back? How have you responded?

Paws and Passages
God's Healing Touch in Grief

The darker the night, the brighter the stars,
The deeper the grief, the closer is God!
FYODOR DOSTOYEVSKY, *CRIME AND PUNISHMENT*

Karen didn't realize how special the experience would be when she got the call from a hospice organization she worked through. They had a request from a fellow in a nursing home. He wanted visits from a therapy dog, but not just any dog. It had to be a collie. Karen had the only collies in the program, so they were contacting her.

Karen's tricolored collie, Rocky, was tapped for the task, and the man loved his visits. Karen took Rocky to see him once a week. His times with the dog seemed to perk him up and, for a while, he seemed to rally. He had not wanted to be at the home, but he started getting more involved in activities there after Rocky entered the picture.

Then one week Karen brought a different therapy dog to see him, a female collie named Raven. The man said Raven was nice, but could Rocky please come back? Not till later did Karen discover the reason for his request. He showed her a photo of a pup he'd had many years before, when his own children were growing up. It was the spitting image of Rocky. No wonder this dog stole his heart!

Eventually the man was moved to a hospice house. Karen and Rocky visited him there on the last evening of his life. He was surrounded by his family and wasn't very coherent, but he petted Rocky all the same. They were only with him for a few minutes. He passed away later that night. Karen and Rocky attended his memorial service at his family's request and were introduced on stage.

Rocky's visits made this man's last six months of life better. In that sense, though he died in the end, Rocky had a healing influence on him. He and Karen are not the first dog and handler therapy team to ease the way for someone whose life is ending.

Gale has also done extensive therapy work with her dogs, including visiting people on hospice. Three or four years after she started, she went through what she calls a "Doubting Thomas" period. She wasn't sure this was what God wanted for her. She prayed for guidance, and He used a hospice patient to provide it.

Gale got a call from a hospice volunteer about a woman who was dying. At an earlier point in her life, she had done some work with wolves. Gale's therapy dog, Mysti, was a Belgian Tervuren and looked a bit wolf-like herself. Gale took Mysti to visit this woman.

The patient had been mostly incoherent. She hadn't been lucid for more than five minutes at a time. When she saw Mysti, she wanted the dog on her bed. Mysti stretched out beside her and she threw her arms around her new canine friend's neck and wept into her fur. She then carried on a coherent 30-minute conversation with Gale all about the wolves. The volunteer was stunned.

Gale and Mysti walked outside. She looked at her dog and looked up at the heavens. "Now I remember why I do this work," she exclaimed. She looks back on this as an incredible healing moment in her own life, and a real turning point.

Gale and Mysti went to see their new friend several more times before she passed away. On their second visit, family members were with her. Once again, the woman carried on a coherent conversation. Her relatives were thrilled, amazed, and grateful. Mysti the dog unlocked something in this woman. She somehow served as a four-pawed bridge to open lines of communication. Her family had moments with their loved one that they might not have had otherwise.

Chris and his therapy dog, Daisy, were able to offer a healing touch to a little girl who was dying of cancer. On their first visit they found her in a beanbag chair. Daisy went over and laid her head on the child's lap, and she put her hand on Daisy's fur. Chris and Daisy visited a total of four or five times. The child's mom went on and on about how much Daisy had helped her daughter, and the whole family.

Chris brought all his therapy dogs—Daisy, Stormy, and Ty—to visit a mother under hospice care. He also got to know the woman's husband and two sons. They were always excited to see the dogs. Those visits helped so much that the family started calling Chris to come over. The visits happened in the woman's home and lasted for two or three hours. Chris and the dogs would spend time with the patient and just let her talk. Afterward they would visit with the family. The husband told Chris that after he left, his wife would talk about the dogs. The visits gave this family a break in the midst of their sadness.

These patients and their families were given a marvelous gift at a critical time in their lives. A dog's loving presence ministered to them in a unique way. A special woman gave Jesus a gift that uniquely ministered to Him not long before His own agonizing death on a cross.

Jesus wasn't sick or in hospice care, but He knew His end was coming. He had returned to Bethany and was attending a dinner in His honor. Mary, sister of Lazarus, anointed Him with a jar of costly perfume, and Judas, the disciple who would soon betray Jesus, didn't like this one bit. He griped that it was a waste of resources; the perfume could have been sold to raise money for the poor. Scripture tells us that in reality, Judas was bummed that he hadn't had a chance to steal the funds for himself. But what was Jesus's reaction?

Jesus defended Mary. In John 12:7-8 (NLT) He said, "Leave her alone. She did this in preparation for my burial. You will always have the poor among you, but you will not always have me."

Jesus knew that in short order, He would be hung on a cross and would die for the sins of the world. He was facing not just physical death, but separation from the Father. He was facing a "passage" from this life so agonizing that He would later sweat drops of blood in anticipation of it. He knew He would be ridiculed and rejected, and even Peter would deny Him. But this woman seemed to "get" what was happening and expressed her love and affection for Him in a lavish fashion. I have to think that warmed His heart and ministered to Him at one of the most excruciating periods in His life. I have to think that Mary's act of love and worship was a healing touch that, though it did not change what He would go through, must have lifted Him, if briefly, and provided a break in His sadness.

Healing touches come in all shapes and sizes, and they don't all cure. Some just lighten the loads we can't escape. Do you know someone facing grief and loss who needs the healing touch of your loving presence today?

The LORD *is close to the brokenhearted and saves those who are crushed in spirit (Psalm 34:18).*

Consider This:

How have you seen a pet or person or the Lord ease the way for someone whose life was ending? Is God calling you to do this for someone in your life?

Meet the Author

M.R. Wells has authored or coauthored six previous devotional books for pet lovers. She has also written extensively for children's television and video programming, including several Disney shows, the animated PBS series *Adventures from the Book of Virtues*, and the action video series *Bibleman*. She shares her Southern California home with the puppies and kitties she adores: Becca, Marley, Mica, Bo, Bonbon, and Brandi.

For more information visit
www.fourpawsfromheaven.com

Four Paws from Heaven
Devotions for Dog Lovers

Life Is Better with a Dog

Friend, family member, guardian, comforter—a dog can add so much to our lives. These furry, four-footed creatures truly are wonderful gifts from a loving Creator to bring joy, laughter, and warmth to our hearts and homes. Sometimes they do seem "heaven sent."

These delightful devotions will make you smile and perhaps grow a little misty as you enjoy true stories of how God watches over and provides for us even as we care for our canine companions. Experience warm moments of connection with Him as you consider

- how a little obedience can keep you from danger
- why trusting your Master is always a good thing to do
- how just being with God is the best possible place to be

Dogs to the Rescue

What Dogs Can Teach Us About Life, Love, and Loyalty

From a coauthor of *Four Paws from Heaven* (more than 125,000 copies sold) comes a devotional for everyone who has ever loved a dog. This collection of short, inspirational stories features service dogs, therapy dogs, and personal pets that have helped their humans in sometimes unexpected ways. Discover

- what dogs can teach us about the care and faithfulness of the Master
- the unusual means God sometimes uses to come to our aid
- what we can learn from dogs about facing life's challenges

These heartwarming tales of dog heroics will teach you that who you are on the inside matters most—and that with God (and a furry friend) on your side, there is no obstacle you can't overcome.

To learn more about Harvest House books and
to read sample chapters, visit our website:

www.harvesthousepublishers.com

HARVEST HOUSE PUBLISHERS
EUGENE, OREGON